Multilingual Testing and Assessment

SECOND LANGUAGE ACQUISITION

Series Editors: **Professor David Singleton**, *University of Pannonia, Hungary* and Fellow Emeritus, *Trinity College, Dublin, Ireland* and **Associate Professor Simone E. Pfenninger**, *University of Salzburg, Austria*

This series brings together titles dealing with a variety of aspects of language acquisition and processing in situations where a language or languages other than the native language is involved. Second language is thus interpreted in its broadest possible sense. The volumes included in the series all offer in their different ways, on the one hand, exposition and discussion of empirical findings and, on the other, some degree of theoretical reflection. In this latter connection, no particular theoretical stance is privileged in the series; nor is any relevant perspective – sociolinguistic, psycholinguistic, neurolinguistic, etc. – deemed out of place. The intended readership of the series includes final-year undergraduates working on second language acquisition projects, postgraduate students involved in second language acquisition research, and researchers, teachers and policymakers in general whose interests include a second language acquisition component.

All books in this series are externally peer-reviewed.

Full details of all the books in this series and of all our other publications can be found on http://www.multilingual-matters.com, or by writing to Multilingual Matters, St Nicholas House, 31-34 High Street, Bristol BS1 2AW, UK.

SECOND LANGUAGE ACQUISITION: 151

Multilingual Testing and Assessment

Gessica De Angelis

MULTILINGUAL MATTERS
Bristol • Blue Ridge Summit

DOI https://doi.org/10.21832/DEANGE0541
Library of Congress Cataloging in Publication Data
A catalog record for this book is available from the Library of Congress.
Names: De Angelis, Gessica, author.
Title: Multilingual Testing and Assessment/Gessica De Angelis.
Description: Bristol, UK; Blue Ridge Summit, PA: Multilingual Matters, 2021. | Series: Second Language Acquisition: 115 | Includes bibliographical references. | Summary: "This book addresses the need for research and guidance on testing multilingual students. The author introduces an integrated approach to testing and assessment; provides guidelines for test-writers, teachers and educators; and demonstrates how to use the integrated approach to testing and assessment in a multilingual educational context"—Provided by publisher.
Identifiers: LCCN 2021015230 (print) | LCCN 2021015231 (ebook) | ISBN 9781800410534 (paperback) | ISBN 9781800410541 (hardback) | ISBN 9781800410558 (pdf) | ISBN 9781800410565 (epub)
Subjects: LCSH: Second language acquisition—Ability testing. | Language and languages—Study and teaching—Foreign speakers—Evaluation. | Language and languages—Ability testing. | Bilingualism in children—Ability testing.
Classification: LCC P118.75 .D43 2021 (print) | LCC P118.75 (ebook) | DDC 404/.20287—dc23 LC record available at https://lccn.loc.gov/2021015230
LC ebook record available at https://lccn.loc.gov/2021015231

British Library Cataloguing in Publication Data
A catalogue entry for this book is available from the British Library.

ISBN-13: 978-1-80041-054-1 (hbk)
ISBN-13: 978-1-80041-053-4 (pbk)

Multilingual Matters
UK: St Nicholas House, 31-34 High Street, Bristol BS1 2AW, UK.
USA: NBN, Blue Ridge Summit, PA, USA.

Website: www.multilingual-matters.com
Twitter: Multi_Ling_Mat
Facebook: https://www.facebook.com/multilingualmatters
Blog: www.channelviewpublications.wordpress.com

Copyright © 2021 Gessica De Angelis.

All rights reserved. No part of this work may be reproduced in any form or by any means without permission in writing from the publisher.

The policy of Multilingual Matters/Channel View Publications is to use papers that are natural, renewable and recyclable products, made from wood grown in sustainable forests. In the manufacturing process of our books, and to further support our policy, preference is given to printers that have FSC and PEFC Chain of Custody certification. The FSC and/or PEFC logos will appear on those books where full certification has been granted to the printer concerned.

Typeset by Deanta Global Publishing Services, Chennai, India
Printed and bound in the UK by the CPI Books Group Ltd.
Printed and bound in the US by NBN.

Contents

	Acknowledgements	vii
1	Multilingual Testing and Assessment	1
	1.1 Introduction	1
	1.2 The Black-and-White Fallacy	3
	1.3 The Terminology Used in This Book	4
	1.4 Overview of the Volume	7
2	Traditional, Holistic and Integrated Approaches to Testing and Assessment	10
	2.1 The Traditional Monolingual Conceptualisation of Language	10
	2.2 The Holistic Conceptualisation of Language	14
	2.3 Towards a Multilingual Construct for Testing and Assessment	18
	2.4 An Integrated Approach to Multilingual Testing and Assessment	26
3	From Bilingual to Multilingual Education	28
	3.1 Strong and Weak Forms of Bilingual Education	29
	3.2 Content and Language Integrated Learning	31
	3.3 CLIL and Assessment	32
	3.4 Multilingual Education	34
	3.5 Is Functional Multilingualism an Achievable Objective?	36
	3.6 How Long Does it Take for Immigrant Children to Reach the Academic Level of Their Native Peers?	44
4	Multilingual Assessment Practices in Education	49
	4.1 Monolingual Testing: Implications for Students, Teachers and Test Developers	49
	4.2 Focusing on Tests	52
	4.3 Focusing on the Test Takers: Grouping by Language Background and Community Languages	62

5	Developing Tests for Multilingual Populations	66
	5.1 Design	68
	5.2 Administration	78
	5.3 Scoring	79
	5.4 Interpretation	80
6	Assessing Multilingual Narratives	83
	6.1 Using Narratives in Linguistics and Education	84
	6.2 Eliciting Narratives	86
	6.3 Measures of Narrative Analysis	88
	6.4 The Multilingual Assessment Instrument for Narratives	93
	6.5 Assessing Multilingual Narratives and the South Tyrol Study	95
7	Multilingual Narratives: The South Tyrol Study	96
	7.1 The Multilingual Context of South Tyrol	96
	7.2 Research Aims and Questions	98
	7.3 Immigrant Population in South Tyrol and Ladin Schools	101
	7.4 Methods	103
	7.5 Results	108
	7.6 Discussion	117
8	Looking Ahead	125
	8.1 Designing Multilingual Tests	126
	8.2 Classifying Multilinguals in Testing	127
	8.3 Multilinguals' Perceptions of Their Own Language Competence	129
	8.4 Monolingual and Multilingual Communication	130
	8.5 Concluding Comment	132
	References	133
	Index	147

Acknowledgements

I thank the Ladin school board, particularly Carla Comploj, for funding the study included in this volume and for providing significant assistance during the data collection in local schools. I would also like to thank the local project coordinator Olimpia Rasom and local collaborators Emanuela Atz and Vigilio Iori. Other collaborators I would like to thank include Roberta Dellantonio, Lois Kastlunger, Sonia Pescosta, Maria Grazia Pitscheider, Elisabeth Sanin, Samantha Scappiti, Angelika Tengler, Isabella Ties, Eveline Vinatzer and Francesca Zulian. Narrative macrostructure was analysed by a team that included myself, Olimpia Rasom and Emanuela Atz. I also thank Dr Simon A. Thomas for his excellent proofreading services and for his patience in reviewing several drafts of this volume.

1 Multilingual Testing and Assessment

1.1 Introduction

The field of multilingual testing and assessment has grown rapidly in recent years due to the widespread need to integrate immigrant populations into mainstream education and provide fair and equitable forms of assessment for all students, regardless of prior language background, educational context and geographical location. Although much progress has been made worldwide, most academic discussions have focused on bilingual speakers and their assessment needs, often in homogeneous educational contexts. Such a narrow emphasis has created a significant gap in testing and assessment research, as most of the available proposals are not conceived for speakers of more than two languages and cannot be easily adopted in multilingual educational contexts. A core aim of this book is to contribute to the development of multilingual testing and assessment research by going beyond bilingualism and extending current discussions to speakers of more than two languages, which may include students with very different language profiles, from recent immigrants with poor language skills to minority language speakers born and raised in multilingual contexts who never moved from their native land.

This volume is intended as a non-technical resource to offer help and guidance to all those who work in education with multilingual populations. At the heart of the considerations expressed is the difference between designing multilingual tests and testing multilingual individuals, a distinction that is addressed throughout the volume through the dichotomy of the test and the test taker. A primary goal is to examine the different approaches used to test multilinguals in education and provide a perspective based on both individual and societal factors, i.e. multilinguals' linguistic background (individual) and the languages spoken in the communities in which they live (societal).

Chapter 1 discusses how current academic discourse is polarised at two extremes that are essentially incompatible with one another. At one end, *traditional* approaches to testing and assessment defend the use of monolingual tests with multiple language speakers, even though the language of testing may be a second language for the test takers. At the other extreme, *holistic* approaches regard monolingual testing as insufficiently inclusive and propose that students' multiple languages become part of the testing process. The use of tests written in multiple languages is, however, not a viable solution when more than two or three languages are involved.

The complexity of designing multilingual tests that are suitable for populations with very diverse language profiles is so vast that the probability of finding a 'one-size-fits-all' solution is remote. This volume proposes to overcome existing barriers through a third approach – the *integrated approach to testing and assessment* – that aims to answer educational questions about students' progress and performance by making use of all relevant and reliable information about the test and the test takers. The underlying assumption is that by combining different types of information, test writers, examiners and educators will be able to make more informed decisions when designing, administering, scoring and interpreting the test results of multilingual populations.

The integrated approach to multilingual testing and assessment is a flexible approach that reflects the fundamental belief that, in most cases, it is not the test that is not suitable but the use that is made of tests in education. All tests can be designed in a way that is sufficiently sensitive to linguistically and culturally diverse student populations, and all tests can be used fairly if due consideration is given to test takers' profiles and their living environment when they are scored and interpreted. The integrated approach to multilingual testing and assessment thus refers to the process of gathering information about the knowledge, skills and abilities of multilingual learners, using tools *designed* for linguistically and culturally diverse populations that may be *administered* in multiple modalities, *scored* by multilingual examiners and *interpreted* using data about the test takers that includes information about their language background and their living environment. Through the careful interpretation of test scores and what they tell us about the test population, the test takers' individual and social dimensions become an integral part of the assessment process, ensuring a fairer and more equitable testing process for all multilinguals.

From these premises, this volume is organised around three main thematic areas. The first introduces the integrated approach to testing and assessment and provides an overview of existing research conducted with multilingual populations (Chapters 2–4). The second offers a number of recommendations for test writers, teachers and educators that aim to outline the steps involved in the design, administration, scoring and interpretation of tests for multiple language speakers (Chapter 5). The third provides an example of formative assessment in a trilingual educational context developed in accordance with the rationale of the integrated approach to testing and assessment. This example is taken from a research study on multilingual narratives conducted with immigrant children (aged 6–14) in trilingual schools in South Tyrol, Italy (Chapters 6 and 7). The volume concludes with some considerations about the integrated approach to testing and assessment and the challenges associated with monitoring students' progress in multilingual contexts (Chapter 8). The remainder of the present chapter discusses the 'Black-and-White Fallacy' in multilingual testing and assessment research (Section 1.2), clarifies the terminology used in the volume (Section 1.3) and provides a chapter-by-chapter outline of the subsequent content (Section 1.4).

1.2 The Black-and-White Fallacy

The proposal of an integrated approach to testing and assessment was motivated by a need to find an approach that would be sufficiently flexible to effectively manage individual variability and different linguistic contexts.

One of the problems in the field of testing and assessment is that academics and test writers tend to think in terms of 'either/or' categories: either a test is monolingual or all the languages of the test takers should be included in the test; either a test is traditional or it is holistic. Either way, black-and-white thinking prevails. Since the use of multiple languages in testing when more than two or three languages are involved is not feasible, and in most cases a multilingual option is far too expensive or time-consuming for schools, suitable alternatives should be explored. The problem, however, is not what each position dictates but the limitations that each position imposes. Although other options may be available, the potential positions are restricted by a Black-and-White Fallacy that prevents us from moving forward.

Last year, I attended a conference on multilingualism with a focus on translanguaging (García, 2009; García & Li Wei, 2014). What struck me most about this conference was not the academic depth of the presentations but the realisation that many teachers and academics also conceptualise multilingualism in terms of either/or categories – either 'monolingualism' or 'translanguaging', with nothing in between. The mind loves to classify and 'pigeonhole' information to fit a small number of restricted categories; the world, however, is not black and white, and multilingualism is certainly an expression of diversity and differences rather than uniformity. In my view, the first step towards a solution is therefore to become more open-minded and think of alternatives in relation to each step of the assessment process. Rather than focusing on how multilinguals use language in their daily lives, we might instead think about who the multilinguals we are testing are, what their learning experience is and how they interact with languages in their daily environment. In sum, multilingualism implies a reality and a way of life that cannot be diluted into two categories, as too many additional variables are involved.

1.3 The Terminology Used in This Book

Multilingual testing and assessment is a relatively young discipline and, as such, some of the terms used in the literature are still contradictory or inconsistent, while the same term may sometimes be used with a narrow or broad focus. In order to avoid interpretive confusion, this section aims to clarify how certain key terms and concepts are used in this book. In particular, attention is paid to the difference between bilingualism and multilingualism, and between evaluation, testing and assessment.

With regard to the difference between bilingualism and multilingualism, it is important to stress from the outset that the field of multilingual testing and assessment is widely informed by the bilingual assessment literature, which has enjoyed a very long tradition in applied linguistics due to the number of bilingual programmes established throughout the world during the 20th century. While this situation has allowed scholars to isolate the most relevant issues for today's multilingual assessment practices and to place academic discussions within well-defined theoretical frameworks, multilinguals and bilinguals remain very different populations with very different requirements and profiles. When these differences are taken into account, questions inevitably arise about the generalisability and feasibility of existing practices, especially since such practices were not originally designed with multilingual populations in mind. Assessing multilingual speakers is undoubtedly more complex and challenging than assessing bilingual speakers, and the lack of a distinction between the two populations is an unfortunate oversimplification that prevents us from asking (and answering) population-specific questions and moving forward.

Multilingualism research is customarily divided into individual and societal multilingualism, which is an initial distinction that must be made in order to understand the complex profiles of multilingual individuals (Aronin & Singleton, 2012). Research on individual multilingualism focuses on the mind and the internal variables that can influence comprehension, production and learning processes, while research on societal multilingualism focuses on social contexts and the role of variables related to the external environment. Researchers working on individual and societal multilingualism use the term 'multilingual(ism)' in different ways due to the different foci of their research. The tendency to use the term to refer to bilingualism and bilingual phenomena is relatively common in societal multilingualism research because the difference between speaker types is typically not essential. By contrast, the difference between speaker types is critical for individual multilingualism research, because the presence or absence of additional knowledge in the mind can significantly speed up or slow down comprehension and production processes and – which is of most relevance to assessment – can lead to different learning outcomes for the individual.

To clarify this point, let us take the example of a school board that wants to know how long it will take for an immigrant student to achieve results similar to those of native peers attending the same school. This is a question about individual learning processes and the speed of learning that cannot be answered by looking at external variables alone. From a language acquisition perspective, we know that the number and type of languages already known determine the speed and quality of learning (Bardel & Falk, 2007; De Angelis, 2019; De Houwer, 2009; Flynn *et al.*, 2004), so the focus on how an individual learns and processes language or academic content through one or more languages, perhaps known at different proficiency levels, cannot be divorced from the number of languages the individual knows. In other words, being bilingual or multilingual can make a substantial difference, so it makes little sense to refer to learners as multilinguals if they are not. The difference between bilingualism and multilingualism is not a mere matter of terminology; it is also a matter of questions that researchers can ask and answer about multilingual student populations. Individual multilingualism research that groups bilinguals and multilinguals into the same subject pool will not be able to address meaningful questions about the speed and quality of learning because of the subject-selection bias that such a large grouping would introduce. Because of the implications and the importance of individual multilingualism for testing and assessment research, this book makes a clear and consistent distinction between bilinguals and multilinguals so that questions specific to multilingual populations can be adequately addressed.

With regard to the terms *evaluation*, *testing* and *assessment*, these are used to distinguish three main areas of research and educational practice. Since several definitions of these terms are available in the literature (see Baird *et al.*, 2017; Davis, 2018; Harlen & James, 1997), a description is given below of how they are used in the current work and their intended referents. As this volume is a non-technical resource, however, this clarification is primarily intended for teachers and educators to distinguish the various types of tests they use in their work.

To begin with the term *evaluation*, this is used to refer to the process of evaluating a structured unit or component that might range from an educational system to an entire programme, course or curriculum. The evaluation process is closely related to its underlying objective of achieving a judgement of effectiveness and providing results that can be used to inform curriculum planning and policymakers.

The terms that are used most frequently in this volume are *testing* and *assessment*. While these terms are sometimes used interchangeably, for instance when referring to testing and assessment as a general process, *testing* is mainly used to refer to all those methods used to measure students' knowledge, skills and abilities and to understand students' progress, while *assessment* is used to refer to the process or procedures involved in gathering information about students' knowledge, skills and abilities by using a range of different methods or tests that enable us to understand what students have learned and still need to learn.

Different types of assessments are used in education, which also differ in purpose and rationale. I will be referring to three main types: formative, summative and diagnostic assessment. The objectives of these three types of assessment are very different and are briefly reviewed below.

Formative assessment is a form of assessment that is sometimes referred to as 'assessment for learning'. It refers to all the methods that teachers use to evaluate students' progress during the school year, i.e. while students are still in the process of learning. Formative assessment is therefore concerned with learning as it happens, so teachers can use this form of assessment for very different purposes. For instance, it can be used to gain an insight into students' learning processes and provide them with feedback that can help them improve their learning, or to identify potential learning problems that need to be addressed through appropriate pedagogical intervention, which may range from individualised remedial strategies to class-wide content reviews. Formative assessment is thus a form of assessment that is used periodically throughout the school year to gather information that can be valuable to the teacher and that she/he can also use for the benefit of students in various ways.

Summative assessment is another core type of assessment that is often referred to as 'assessment of learning'. It is typically administered at the end of a learning cycle and its main purpose is to assess students' overall achievements up to a specific point in time. A typical example would be a test given at the end of the school year or of a course. Summative assessment therefore measures whether, at the end of an instructional cycle – which could be a unit, a term or a school year – learning objectives have been achieved. Teachers generally use well-defined assessment criteria that can be introduced to students before the test, provided the latter are old enough to understand them, so that expectations and requirements are clearly defined. With this assessment, students' performance is graded and this determines whether the student can continue to study at the next level.

A third type of assessment is diagnostic assessment, which is a form of assessment that is mainly associated with tests given to students before classes begin. Tests can be administered for a wide range of reasons, from classroom placement to the identification of learning disabilities. The interpretation of diagnostic assessment is very broad and this volume does not distinguish between special needs and classroom placement as the distinction is not relevant to the discussions presented. Diagnostic assessment can be used to assess students' knowledge and understanding of a subject, such as knowledge of the language of instruction or, when students move from other schools or countries, knowledge already acquired in a particular subject, for example mathematics. Diagnostic assessment is therefore widely used to identify individual areas of strength or weakness, the presence or absence of knowledge and skills that might be necessary for the successful completion of a course, the existence of learning disabilities and so forth.

While assessment, testing and evaluation differ considerably in purpose and use, they have substantial implications for multilingual student populations, particularly immigrant and minority language speakers with low proficiency in the official language(s) of instruction. Some of these implications may be undesirable and detrimental to learning, while others can be constructive and helpful. Formative assessment, for instance, can be a constructive and valuable tool for teachers who want to understand students' progress and identify those who are falling behind. Immigrant and minority language students are likely to derive great benefit from the use of individualised pedagogical intervention while they are still in the process of learning rather than at the end of the school year. Moreover, individualised feedback can also be used to improve communication with students' families and help parents become actively involved in a child's learning progress. Children may be assigned additional language activities to complete at home, for instance, which would be based on their actual learning needs rather than hypothetical needs. In contrast, other forms of assessment may be discriminatory in nature or can be used either to the benefit or the detriment of immigrant and minority language populations. For example, summative assessment, and norm-reference tests in particular, raise grave concerns when used with students who have little or low proficiency in the language of testing due to the potential repercussions for progress and advancement. Diagnostic tests can be highly beneficial for recently arrived immigrants but can also be used unwisely, for instance when schools use them to set up classes that isolate immigrant children from their peers.

1.4 Overview of the Volume

Following this introductory chapter, which provides details of the book's general aims and objectives and clarifies the terminology used in the volume, Chapter 2 introduces the reader to the distinction between traditional and holistic approaches to testing and assessment, explaining how they have influenced testing practices over the years and the kind of limitations they pose for further theoretical developments today. After considering the advantages and disadvantages of each approach, Chapter 2 provides an initial description of the integrated approach to multilingual testing and assessment as a third option that aims to be a mediating position between traditional and holistic approaches which, it is claimed, is best suited to a wider range of linguistically and culturally diverse student populations.

Chapter 3 provides an overview of the main types of bilingual and multilingual programmes available worldwide, devoting attention to their aims and objectives and, where possible, their degree of success. As the multilingual testing and assessment literature is largely based on bilingual education and assessment, this chapter begins with a brief summary of bilingual education, including its beginnings and development, and how it paved the way for the introduction of multilingual education programmes in different geographical contexts. This review begins with a discussion of the strong and weak forms of bilingual education that originated mainly in Canada and the United States, before moving on to an introduction of content and language integrated learning (CLIL) education in European contexts. The remainder of the chapter is devoted to multilingual education programmes in Europe and their unique association with minority language populations and multilingual sociolinguistic settings.

Chapter 4 provides an overview of the kind of research that has been carried out to improve assessment practices in recent years and make them more suitable for multilingual students attending school in different educational contexts. The types of adjustments and changes introduced are classified according to the dichotomy of the test and the test taker, i.e. those changes aimed at improving tests and those aimed at classifying test takers according to their personal background and linguistic profiles. The types of adjustments and modifications examined concern the use of bilingual and multilingual scoring rubrics, the introduction of bilingual test instructions, the possibility of answering in multiple languages and the use of test accommodation strategies and techniques such as simplification, translation and the use of the first language. Examples of research in each category and their effectiveness are also discussed.

Chapter 5 further explains the integrated approach to testing and assessment by providing step-by-step non-technical recommendations to writing tests for linguistically and culturally diverse student populations. The aim is to provide a general framework for test development and test interpretation that can be easily used by teachers, test writers and educators working with multilingual students. The recommendations are organised into four main thematic areas: design, administration, scoring and interpretation. The overall objective is to raise awareness of what can be done to improve assessment practices during each stage of test development and the type of options available at each stage of the process. Progress monitoring questions are also included in each section to further guide the test writing process.

Chapter 6 is devoted to the literature on multilingual narratives. Narratives are oral accounts of real or imaginary events that are widely used in educational and clinical settings to assess children's language and cognitive development and to identify children with specific language impairments (SLI). Multilingual narratives are valuable tools for assessment as they reflect how children conceptualise, plan and organise content, using both language and cognitive skills. Like most of the literature on multilingual assessment, most research studies have focused on bilingual child language development and bilingualism. To the best of my knowledge, however, narrative studies in three or more languages that examine linguistic and cognitive development from a multilingual perspective are not yet available.

Knowledge of how narrative abilities may develop in languages known at different proficiency levels is essential to deepen our understanding of the association between developing the cognitive ability to structure a story and developing enough language to complete a narrative task. This volume includes a review of the literature on narratives because it uses a study on multilingual narratives as an example of how the integrated approach to testing and assessment can be used in multilingual education (see Chapter 7). This study was conducted with immigrant children (aged 6–14) attending schools in the trilingual Ladin educational system in South Tyrol, Italy.

Chapter 6 introduces research on multilingual narratives and discusses the challenges associated with the evaluation of multilingual narratives in children. The overall aim is to discuss research on bilingual and multilingual narratives, examine how narratives can be elicited in multiple languages and identify the instruments that can be used. The most frequently used narrative production measures are also explored and the Multilingual Assessment Instrument for Narratives (MAIN) (Gagarina *et al.*, 2012) is reviewed.

Chapter 7 aims to show how the integrated approach to testing and assessment works in practice through a study of multilingual narratives conducted in South Tyrol. The chapter explains how immigrant children were tested, how the test was designed and the types of measures that were used for assessment. The focus is on how immigrant children and local minority language speakers born and raised in the region develop narrative abilities in multiple languages and on the level of language competence required to carry out narrative tasks in different languages. Explicit reference is made to the *recommendations* presented in Chapter 5 and to each phase of the assessment process (design, administration, scoring and interpretation).

Chapter 8, the concluding chapter, provides a brief summary of the key proposals presented in the volume and of the issues related to designing multilingual tests and classifying multilinguals in testing. The chapter also explores the role of testing in shaping multilinguals' perception of their own language competence and the place of a monolingual–multilingual continuum in human communication.

2 Traditional, Holistic and Integrated Approaches to Testing and Assessment

The primary aim of this chapter is to provide an overview of traditional and holistic approaches to testing and assessment and to examine how they have influenced testing practices over the years. The rationale behind the integrated approach is also introduced, along with an initial explanation of the type of flexibility it can offer.

Traditional and *holistic* approaches to testing and assessment reflect fundamentally different ways of conceptualising what language is and how it should be tested in education (Gorter & Cenoz, 2017; Kramsch, 2012; López *et al.*, 2016, 2017; Poza, 2017; Shohamy, 2011). The review of each approach includes a description of its origins, the academic debates that have developed around it, its current use in educational contexts and its suitability for bilingual and multilingual student populations. A third option is then introduced – the *integrated approach to testing and assessment* – which is a more flexible and comprehensive alternative that, it will be argued, is suitable for a broader range of linguistically and culturally diverse student populations.

The chapter explores these topics in more detail and the content is organised as follows. It begins with a review of the traditional (Section 2.1) and holistic (Section 2.2) conceptualisations of language and the implications of each approach for testing and assessment. This is followed by a discussion of the multilingual construct for assessment (Section 2.3) and a brief introduction of the integrated approach to testing and assessment (Section 2.4).

2.1 The Traditional Monolingual Conceptualisation of Language

Traditional approaches to testing and assessment are based on the view that every language is an independent unit of knowledge and is therefore independent of other languages in the mind. This conceptualisation of language is a monolingual construct that represents the dominant theoretical position of most applied linguistics and educational research. For decades, researchers and educators have conceived and treated languages as autonomous units of knowledge, and thus as closed and intact systems with well-defined boundaries between them. The influence of this perspective has been so pervasive that it has influenced the way languages have been learned, taught and evaluated for a very long time (Gorter & Cenoz, 2017; López et al., 2016; Poza, 2017; Shohamy, 2011). Even today, most researchers and educators find it difficult to conceptualise language and language boundaries in any other way.

Decades of second language (L2) research show that most scholars, having embraced this idea that languages exist in isolation from other languages in the mind and develop independently, posit that native-like proficiency is the ultimate goal of language development. Theoretical arguments have focused either on the speed and rate of development of individual languages or on aspects of language acquisition at a single point in time, but the existence of boundaries between languages has typically been accepted and rarely questioned.

The stance of conceptualising languages as independent units of knowledge has enabled researchers to examine and understand important differences between the ways adults and children learn the first language (L1) and the L2 (Clark, 2016; Cook, 2016; Gass & Selinker, 2008; Lust & Foley, 2004; Mitchell et al., 2013; Myles, 2010; Saville-Troike & Barto, 2017) and to gain valuable insights into the role of background languages in the learning process (Unsworth, 2016). Even researchers who have focused on multilingualism have mostly embraced the monolingual construct as their default theoretical position and, while attention was extended to the presence of more than two languages in the mind, languages remained conceived as self-contained systems that could be added to the individual's language repertoire, thereby becoming a third language (L3) or an additional language (Ln) (Bardel & Falk, 2007; Jarvis & Pavlenko, 2008; Puig-Mayenco et al., 2020; Ringbom, 2007).

The monolingual construct is recognisable in many areas of applied linguistics and educational research, and several examples can be mentioned from very diverse fields of enquiry, such as cross-linguistic influence (CLI), classroom communication, L2 pedagogy, minority language survival or testing and assessment.

To begin with research on CLI, the monolingual construct is clearly noticeable in the way transfer is conceived and treated in research. Transfer is seen as a phenomenon that occurs between two languages, regardless of the number of languages the speaker knows. Transfer can go backward and forward and can be multidirectional, but it is usually limited to the interaction between two intact language systems (De Angelis & Dewaele, 2011; Jarvis & Pavlenko, 2008; Ringbom, 2007). A partial exception to this view is the notion of combined CLI, a form of transfer linked to multiple sources but with the target language still viewed as an intact system (De Angelis, 2007, 2019).

Within the field of education, languages are usually taught as independent subjects and, even in bilingual and multilingual programmes, the separation between languages tends to remain in place. In schools, languages are offered at specific times of the day, and there is usually one teacher for each language, or a teacher can teach more than one language but at different times of the day (Gorter & Cenoz, 2017). Language textbooks are also typically monolingual, unless they are intentionally designed for a specific market. This is the case, for instance, with textbooks written for the English-Spanish student market in the United States or for large commercial markets such as those of English or Chinese native speakers. Bilingual textbooks for these markets may show instructions and/or grammar in one language and content in the target language, but the division between languages remains clear.

The monolingual construct also strongly dominates classroom communication and language teaching practices. Most pedagogical approaches to language teaching encourage the use of the target language for classroom interactions, in which students can practice with other students or with the language teacher and learn through real-life communication. It is believed that the use of the target language improves students' overall learning experience and promotes language acquisition (Ellis & Shintani, 2014; Richards & Rodgers, 2001). Even though the use of the L1 is typically discouraged, some scholars remain in favour of its deployment, arguing it can significantly improve communication within the classroom. Cook (2001), for instance, claims that the L1 can be a very useful resource for both students and teachers to facilitate the communication of concepts that are particularly difficult to understand, as well as for complex explanations. Regardless of whether or not the L1 is used in the classroom in addition to the target language, however, what these practices have in common is an underlying rationale driven by a traditional monolingual conceptualisation of language, as a clear separation between the L1 and the L2 remains firmly in place.

Gorter and Cenoz (2017) argue that the practice of language separation in education is also connected to the idea that such separation protects minority languages, ensuring the survival of the language among its speakers. Language mixing and code-switching are not usually supported in the school context because these practices tend to encourage the use of stronger languages at the expense of weaker ones, which would be lost or considerably weakened if they were not used frequently. Tolerance towards language mixing and code-switching is, however, constantly increasing, due to the growing influence of translanguaging approaches to classroom instruction, which see language mixing as a useful pedagogical tool that reflects the way bilinguals naturally use their languages in communication (García, 2009; García & Li Wei, 2014).

The monolingual construct has also strongly influenced the field of testing and assessment, with substantial implications for multilingual student populations. Teachers and test developers are traditionally used to thinking in terms of language-specific assessment practices and rarely consider testing students using a test designed in more than one language. Standardised tests are typical examples of tests designed in one language. Large-scale tests such as the Programme for International Student Assessment (PISA) are translated into other languages, but the test itself is provided in a single language. Students are equally led to think that languages are isolated units of knowledge that need to be tested in isolation from other languages and that they must perform according to the standards of an ideal 'native speaker norm'.

The native speaker norm has been widely criticised in L2 research, particularly in relation to L2 learners and bilingual student populations (Cook, 1997; Grosjean, 1985, 1989, 1992; Kachru, 1994). This wave of criticism is often referred to as the *monolingual bias* in L2 research (Baker & Jones, 1998; Bley-Vroman, 1983; Cook, 1995, 1997; De Angelis & Selinker, 2001; Grosjean, 1992, 2001), a type of bias associated with the practice of measuring L2 learners' performance using native-like norms. The fundamental argument is that if an ideal monolingual norm is used as the main performance benchmark, multiple language speakers will inevitably emerge as poor performers as they cannot easily achieve native-like standards in an L2. As a result, they will be heavily penalised for their rich and diverse language background, sending the negative message that knowledge of multiple languages is not an advantage but a liability (Shohamy, 2011).

Monolingual tests also carry additional implications outside of the classroom, as they can reflect national political ideologies and support political agendas unfavourable to linguistically and culturally diverse populations (Dendrinos, 2019; López *et al.*, 2016; Shohamy, 2007, 2011; Stavans & Hoffmann, 2015). Monolingual tests are being increasingly used for citizenship purposes (Milani, 2008), for example, and 'as tools for denying residence, entrance to educational institutions and the workplace' (Shohamy, 2007: 126).

The monolingual construct thus permeates the way language has been conceptualised and treated in several fields of enquiry over a very long period of time with different and important implications for multiple language speakers, whose rich language backgrounds have often been seen as a problem rather than a resource. A widespread feeling of injustice and unfairness motivated many researchers to systematically reconsider the way languages are conceptualised, treated and used for assessment purposes in education, and holistic approaches to testing and assessment seemed to offer a happy medium between safeguarding the rights and needs of individual learners and maintaining quality in testing. As we shall see, however, holistic assessment, as currently conceptualised, may be well intended but is not very feasible as regards its application.

2.2 The Holistic Conceptualisation of Language

Holistic conceptualisations of language view the co-existence of languages in the mind from a unified perspective. Great emphasis is placed on how multiple language speakers use their languages to communicate in everyday life, mixing languages fluidly without imposing strict boundaries between them. From these considerations of patterns of language use, it is then argued that multiple languages should become part of the assessment process, as this would reflect the way multilinguals naturally use their languages in communication. Holistic approaches to testing and assessment thus object to all those practices that do not pay attention to language diversity and minority language speakers' practices and do not seek to give access to multiple language resources or to integrate the use of multiple languages into testing.

Holistic approaches are relatively new in the field of multilingual testing and assessment while holistic arguments, which are closely related to the much broader *multilingual turn* in applied linguistics, have been put forward in several other areas of enquiry for a very long time. The *multilingual turn* in applied linguistics is a paradigm shift typically associated with research in L2 acquisition and L2 development, where holistic perspectives are generally considered highly innovative because they challenge the traditional monolingual assumptions on which the entire field of L2 research has based its theoretical thinking for decades (Kramsch, 2012). Researchers working in these areas have openly questioned the assumptions underlying some of the key notions associated with L2 knowledge and L2 learning, such as the native/non-native speaker dichotomy, the view of the L2 learner as an incomplete or deficient speaker, the concepts of ultimate attainment and fossilisation, and the nature of L2 knowledge and L2 processing (Dagenais *et al.*, 2007; Makoni & Pennycook, 2012; May, 2014; McLaughlin, 2016; Ortega, 2013; Sembiante, 2016). Over time, these academic debates have contributed to a profound change in L2 research and influenced the way scholars view language, including how they conceive language boundaries and the role of previously acquired languages in facilitating or hindering the acquisition of additional languages.

The literature is filled with debates on the best way to explain the integrated nature of knowledge in the mind and how to account for the social and the individual dimension of the language learner. With special reference to multilingualism, Cenoz (2013) argues for the need to conceptualise multilinguals by focusing on three distinct levels: (1) the learner, (2) the speaker's linguistic repertoire and (3) the context. The focus on the learner is intended to emphasise that it is only by focusing on the individual that 'we can obtain deeper knowledge of the different types of L3 learners and the effects of their prior linguistic knowledge' (Cenoz, 2013: 81) on learning processes. The second emphasises the need to consider the speaker's entire language repertoire rather than individual languages in the mind. The third advocates a usage-based position in that it argues that context should be considered as an essential component of multilingualism research because this allows us to 'to show how the L3 is incorporated into the multilingual speaker's language practices' (Cenoz, 2013: 82). The author's holistic approach was not proposed with multilingual testing and assessment in mind, but as a more general approach to the study of multilingualism.

Over the years, several holistic theories have discussed the relationship between the individual and social dimensions, and some of them are now widely accepted by the research community, such as translanguaging (García, 2009; García & Li Wei, 2014), the Language Mode Hypothesis (Grosjean, 1989, 2001), multicompetence (Cook, 1991, 1992, 1995, 2015), Chaos and Complexity Theory (Larsen-Freeman, 1997, 2011) and Dynamic Systems Theory (Herdina & Jessner, 2002).

2.2.1 Translanguaging

One of the better-known holistic conceptualisations of language is associated with translanguaging theory, which considers multilinguals' language mixing practices as an expression of a unified language repertoire (García, 2009; García & Li Wei, 2014). Translanguaging is an approach to the study of language strongly rooted in bilingualism and sociolinguistics research which is defined as the 'deployment of a speaker's full linguistic repertoire without regard for watchful adherence to the socially and politically defined boundaries of named (and usually national and state) languages' (Otheguy *et al.*, 2015: 281). Poza (2017) traced the origin of the term to Cen Williams' doctoral dissertation submitted to the University of Wales in 1994; García (2009) then used it a few years later to refer to pedagogical strategies for bilingual English–Spanish students in the US contexts. The term is now widely used in education and sociolinguistic research with special reference to immigrants and minority language speakers.

Even though the use of the term translanguaging is now well established and widely understood in education, multilingual communication practices have attracted the attention of many other researchers over the years and a variety of competing terms have also been proposed. Poza (2017) identifies several terms that approximate the idea of translanguaging, such as *flexible bilingualism* (Creese & Blackledge, 2011), *hybrid language practices* (Gutiérrez *et al.*, 1999), *polylingual languaging* (Jørgensen, 2008), *transidiomatic practices* (Jacquemet, 2005), *codemeshing* (Young & Martinez, 2011), *translingual practices* (Canagarajah, 2012) and *metrolingualism* (Otsuji & Pennycook, 2010). While these terms present some degree of variation in their interpretation of multilingual communication practices, the underlying idea they all share is that multiple language speakers use the languages in their repertoire flexibly and fluidly in communication, as translanguaging also postulates.

2.2.2 The Language Mode Hypothesis

The Language Mode Hypothesis (Grosjean, 1985, 1992) is a theory developed in the 1980s with bilingualism and bilingual competence in mind. It was originally motivated by the need to explain how the bilingual mind responds to the external environment in communication. On the basis of Grosjean's (1992: 55) now famous statement that 'a bilingual is NOT the sum of two complete or incomplete monolinguals; rather, he or she has a unique and specific linguistic configuration' (capitalised in the original), he convincingly argued against the tendency to explain bilingual phenomena through a monolingual lens and maintained that bilinguals needed to be viewed as individuals in their own right. His Language Mode Hypothesis introduced the idea that bilinguals are always at some point along a monolingual–bilingual continuum, whose position depends on several external factors such as who they are speaking to, the context and the purpose of communication. At one end of the continuum, the bilingual is in a monolingual mode, communicating in one language and deactivating the language not in use; at the other, the bilingual is in a bilingual mode, switching freely between languages when speaking with another bilingual interlocutor. Bilinguals can also position themselves anywhere along the continuum, depending on the interlocutor's language background, the context and the type of communication.

2.2.3 Multicompetence

Another influential and well-known holistic theory that accounts for the presence of two or more languages in the mind is Cook's (1991, 1992, 1995) notion of multicompetence, which was originally proposed to contrast the idea of monocompetence. Cook had noticed that scholars were referring to either the L1 or the L2 but never to both at the same time. Since there was no term to refer to the co-existence of the L1 and an interlanguage in the mind, he proposed the term 'multicompetence' to describe the state of integration of language knowledge in the mind. At the time, Cook (1992: 585) argued that 'at one level, multicompetence is undeniable; as L2 users do not have two heads, their mind must be different at some level of abstraction' and initially defined the concept as the 'compound state of a mind with two grammars' (Cook, 1991: 112). In his more recent publications, Cook (2015) further elaborates on his ideas, arguing that multicompetence views the L2 user as a whole person with their entire language repertoire. His latest definition describes multicompetence as 'the overall system of a mind or a community that uses more than one language' (Cook, 2015: 2), thus capturing the individual and social dimensions at the same time.

2.2.4 Chaos and Complexity Theory

In the late 1990s, Diane Larsen-Freeman (1997) published a seminal paper on chaos and complexity theory in *Applied Linguistics*, which is now acknowledged to have led to one of the most significant shifts in thinking in L2 acquisition and, more broadly, in applied linguistics in recent decades. In her 1997 article, Larsen-Freeman explained that the study of chaos is not a new concept in the sciences and that her paper was initially motivated by the observation that the process of language acquisition shared several similarities with complex non-linear systems and their functioning. Complex non-linear systems are systems that show several distinctive features. Firstly, they are flexible, dynamic and open to change. Secondly, and more importantly, they can change and adapt by way of interaction with other components through a mechanism of internal reorganisation. Larsen-Freeman argues that the term 'complex' is used for two main reasons which may not be immediately obvious to those approaching the theory for the first time. The first – and perhaps the more understandable – reason is associated with the presence of several different components, a concept she explains by means of the example of a brain that contains billions of neurons. The second and more central reason is that each component is constantly interacting with, and reacting and adjusting to, changes occurring to other components, triggering a process of self-regulation. As she further explains, 'chaos refers simply to the period of complete randomness that complex nonlinear systems enter into irregularly and unpredictably' (Larsen-Freeman, 1997: 143). In complex non-linear systems, the cause–effect relationship is unbalanced because the effect is typically disproportionate in relation to the original cause. That is to say, complex non-linear systems behave predictably up to a certain point, after which their behaviour becomes totally unpredictable. An effective metaphor that Larsen-Freeman provides is that of an avalanche (the effect) that can be caused by a rolling pebble (the cause). In this case, the cause is a small event that triggers a disproportionate and unpredictable effect.

After decades of theoretical thinking about L2 learning based on ordered and predictable input and output categories and the view that learning is a linear process, one can begin to appreciate how chaos and complexity theory became an earthquake that rocked the field of applied linguistics, bringing a much needed and welcome change to the discipline. The times were clearly ready for new directions. Most linguists were beginning to perceive the limitations of the monolingual construct in their work and were eager to break away from theories that lacked adequate explanatory power for the range of phenomena observed in L2 research. Theories that embraced inclusion, diversity and individual differences more systematically represented a step towards more coherent explanations of the language learning process and of the interaction between the social and individual dimensions.

2.2.5 The Dynamic Model of Multilingualism (DMM)

The state of integrated knowledge in the mind is further reflected in the work of Herdina and Jessner (2002), who argue that multilingual language development must be seen from a holistic perspective, as language systems constantly interact and influence each other in language development and use. Herdina and Jessner (2002) propose the DMM – a model that applies Dynamic System Theory to multilingual language development. The DMM explains language development by combining individual and social factors and showing how they are dynamically interconnected in shaping the developmental process. An example of the application of the DMM to written language development can be found in De Angelis and Jessner (2012), who used the model to discuss the written data of trilingual students attending schools in multilingual South Tyrol, Italy. The study showed the dynamic interaction between learners' language systems, providing broad support for Cummins' (1979a, 1979b) Interdependence Hypothesis, which claims the existence of an underlying common proficiency in multiple language speakers. In a recent publication, de Bot (2017) highlighted the similarities between Complexity Theory and Dynamic System Theory. Arguing that the two theories refer to very similar phenomena, he proposed the use of Complex Dynamic Systems Theory to better capture the richness that both these dynamic approaches can offer.

2.3 Towards a Multilingual Construct for Testing and Assessment

A multilingual construct for testing and assessment has not been adequately defined due to the relatively young literature on the topic and a general shortage of studies involving truly multilingual populations. To arrive at a better understanding of this construct, it may be useful to explore and interpret how multilingualism is conceived by different scholars in the field.

2.3.1 Monolingual perspectives seem to endure in most conceptualisations of multilingualism

The term multilingualism is normally employed to refer to and describe students, test takers, programmes and assessment procedures of various kinds, but its use is often inconsistent and seems to be deeply rooted in the traditional conceptualisation of language as a close and intact system.

To begin with purely morphological considerations, it should not be a matter of contention that the prefix 'multi-' implies the existence of several components – in this case, several languages – while the prefix 'bi-' refers to the existence of two parts, i.e. two languages. The former has been used in well-known theoretical concepts in applied linguistics. The notion of *multi*competence, for instance, was originally coined to contrast the idea of *mono*competence and was motivated by the need to capture the presence of more than one language in the mind. While multicompetence was initially coined to refer to the existence of two languages in the mind, it is now broadly understood to refer to the presence of multiple languages in the mind.

The notion of translanguaging makes use of the prefix 'trans-', meaning 'across' or 'beyond', but in order to go across or beyond something, one needs at least two components. The term translanguaging (see definition in Section 2.2.1) is argued to go beyond language boundaries and traditional conceptualisation of language, but the term is broadly used to refer to language mixing behaviour that can only come into existence whenever two or more languages co-exist in the same mind.

The choice of using the prefix 'multi-' (or 'trans-') seems to suggest the co-presence of languages in the mind, which are therefore conceptualised as having some degree of separation between them, or else mixing or merging could not come into existence. It seems to me, then, that the traditional monolingual conceptualisation of language as an individual entity continues to survive in these concepts and be deeply rooted in the idea of multiple parts (languages) forming part of a whole.

The use of the terms *holistic* and *multilingual* also suggests that a close association is being made between the two constructs to the extent that one has come to be naturally connected to the other. A multilingual construct is widely understood to be a holistic one as well, but an assumption of closeness between these two constructs is inappropriate and may alter the interpretation of multilingual phenomena. One example of where the holistic and multilingual constructs do not coincide can be identified in the widespread argument that holistic approaches to testing and assessment should reflect the way multilinguals naturally use their languages in communication. The argument that, since multilinguals constantly mix their languages, tests should integrate the languages students speak, is to some extent contradictory, as language mixing or code-switching behaviour is only *one* of the ways multilinguals use their languages to communicate in real life, as the Language Mode Hypothesis (Grosjean, 1985, 1992) also posits. While it is true that multiple language speakers frequently engage in mixing and code-switching behaviour, it is also true that under certain circumstances they operate in a monolingual mode and decide to function monolingually whenever it is appropriate for them to do so. For multilingual speakers, monolingual communication can be just as natural as language mixing or code-switching, and all these communicative behaviours are part of how a multilingual person functions and communicates in real life. A holistic approach that *selectively* focuses on language mixing and code-switching behaviour, while disregarding the monolingual practices in which multilinguals also engage, cannot be said to be truly holistic, as it only considers certain manifestations of multilingual behaviour rather than the full range of possibilities.

2.3.2 The bilingual bias in multilingualism research

The way multilingualism is conceptualised is also greatly influenced by the presence of a widespread bilingual bias in multilingualism research. The *bilingual bias* refers to the tendency to establish an equivalence between a bilingual and a multilingual mind, which leads to the assumption that the mind functions in the same way regardless of the number of languages the speaker knows. The position blurs the boundaries between speaker types and implies that language knowledge, regardless of type, quality or quantity, does not affect the mind's functioning in any way. The position also generates a Black-and-White Fallacy (see Section 1.2) as the tendency to classify individuals, characteristics or events into either/or categories (in this case monolingual or multilingual) excludes the possibility that other categories may also exist.

As pointed out in Chapter 1, the difference between bilingualism and multilingualism is not merely a matter of terminological preference or schools of thought, but of questions that researchers can ask (and answer) about multilingual populations and multilingual phenomena. By blurring differences between speaker types, it is inevitable that some questions can no longer be asked. For instance, many teachers and school boards want to understand the association between speed of learning and prior language background, asking questions to this end such as 'How long does it take for immigrant children to reach the academic level of their native peers?' To answer this question, it is essential that we use information such as whether the learner has knowledge of one, two or five languages, what type of languages they are, how distant they are from the language(s) of instruction and the level of proficiency the learner has achieved in each language. By blurring speaker types, however, the question cannot be addressed, because downplaying the role of prior language knowledge in the mind implies a lack of recognition that prior language knowledge affects the language learning process in meaningful ways.

The assumption of an identity between the bilingual and the multilingual mind reminds us of past discussions about the monolingual bias in L2 research (see Baker & Jones, 1998; Bley-Vroman, 1983; Cook, 1995, 1997; De Angelis & Selinker, 2001; Grosjean, 1992, 2001). It may be recalled that several scholars have objected to the use of an ideal speaker-hearer norm in research (Grosjean, 1992), but if the bilingual speaker is now taken to be the new 'norm' in multilingualism research, history is bound to repeat itself and for very similar reasons.

A core aim of multilingualism research is to understand and describe the process of language learning and the way language knowledge is organised in the mind, including how it gradually adapts to changes in proficiency level in any of the languages known to the speaker. The question is how learning processes can be adequately described and students' learning assessed if the presence of language knowledge that triggers change in the mind is not explicitly recognised. Everyone can understand that a speaker of five languages is not the equivalent of a speaker of two languages and, as Cook (2015: 283) rightly says, 'to understand what is new, one needs to understand how it differs from what is old'. Hence, we will never be able to understand the multilingual mind (the new) until we conceive it as the old (the bilingual mind).

The bilingual bias can be identified in several areas of research, including the one that concerns us the most here: multilingual testing and assessment. Tests for bilingual speakers are inevitably easier to design, administer and score than those for multilingual speakers, and viewing the field of multilingual testing and assessment through the lens of bilingualism sets conceptual limits that prevent us from devising approaches that are truly inclusive and equitable. The literature on multilingual testing and assessment shows clear arguments in favour of the need to differentiate between monolingual and bilingual or minority language speakers, but very few arguments can be found for the same need in relation to bilingual and multilingual speakers. I have argued for more than a decade that conceptualising the multilingual mind as a mind with two languages 'to which some more languages can be added (or dropped)' but where 'the addition (or reduction) of languages is somewhat optional' (De Angelis, 2007: 15) is a narrow view that prevents us from developing theories that are conceived for speakers who are truly multilingual. The field of multilingual testing and assessment cannot address the needs of the range of multiple language speakers filling today's classrooms or offer advice on how they should be assessed in education if the focus of academic discussions remains restricted to bilingual students and their educational and testing needs.

A comprehensive theory of multilingual testing and assessment must provide a clear rationale for the development of assessment practices that are suitable for both bilingual and multilingual populations. Test takers need to be conceived as multilinguals with diverse cultural and linguistic needs who experience multiple languages in their daily lives through work, school, the community and the family environment. Multilinguals, however, should not become the new norm, as bilinguals and multilinguals may have different profiles and therefore different requirements. A test written for a homogeneous bilingual population can, and should, be very different from one conceived for students with very diverse language backgrounds, as will be explored in more detail in Chapter 5.

Even though holistic approaches to testing and assessment have challenged practices based on traditional monolingual views of language and the outcome of this process has been a major step forward for the field as a whole, the bilingual bias is still preventing us from moving forward. We should not lose sight of the fact that holistic approaches have yet to deliver viable solutions for students who are familiar with more than two languages and that the different types of multilingual speakers also need to be accounted for in testing, as is discussed in the following section.

2.3.3 Who are the multilinguals we are testing?

Most academic discussions of multilingual testing and assessment focus on immigrant students and the difficulties they encounter during the assessment process, which are typically due to low proficiency in the language of testing. The main line of argument is that traditional monolingual assessment practices place these populations at a disadvantage because, due to their poor language skills, such practices do not allow them to show what they have learned. For these reasons, holistic approaches widely call for the inclusion of all the languages that students use in everyday communication, maintaining that in this way these practices can become 'more construct valid, as they enable the manifestation of fuller knowledge in integrated ways, [...] highlighting the advantages, rather than the problems, that multilingual users possess' (Shohamy, 2011: 418).

The need to be fair to the many multilingual immigrants and minority language speakers who have poor knowledge of the language of testing is in no way questioned in this volume, but one cannot lose sight of the fact that many multilinguals are not recent immigrants and do not have great difficulties with the language(s) of instruction. In many bilingual and multilingual sociolinguistic contexts, children live in close contact with people who use different languages in everyday life. In these contexts, the core of the multilingual student population is not composed of children who have difficulties with the language(s) of instruction but of those who are raised speaking minority and majority languages simultaneously and who learn to master them to a high level of fluency. The potential multilingual population is therefore not of a single type; it may include recent immigrants with little knowledge of the languages of instruction and minority language speakers, including dialect speakers, who have grown up speaking several languages and feel totally at ease with the languages of instruction and therefore with the language(s) of testing. Given the range of potential profiles, it is essential that assessment practices are designed for all multilinguals, not just a subset of the student population. The profile we should be concerned with, therefore, is that of a multilingual speaker who may be an immigrant with language difficulties, a local bilingual or trilingual with high fluency in the languages of testing, and anyone else in between. In other words, to make real progress it is essential to start thinking inclusively and focus on what all these types of speakers have in common, as they all represent our potential test takers.

In the literature, we frequently find that the term *minority language speaker* is used to refer to those for whom the language of instruction is an L2. This term makes a clear distinction between those who speak a minority language and those who belong to majority language groups. Minority language speakers, however, are not a homogeneous group and include several subgroups of speakers with completely different characteristics. Today's immigrants, for example, may come from backgrounds that are wealthy and privileged or poor and disadvantaged, or any other intermediate circumstances. Minority language children of recent immigration may enter school without knowledge of the language(s) of instruction or with poor language skills. The term is also used to refer to those who belong to long-established bilingual or multilingual ethnic communities. In this case, children are raised speaking two or more languages from birth or from a very young age.

If we take the multilingual context of South Tyrol, Italy, and Ladin schools as an example – though the same applies to most bilingual and multilingual contexts – we can identify at least two large subgroups of multilingual speakers in schools: the local Ladin L1 children and the children with an immigrant background. Local Ladin children share a number of characteristics. They are typically Ladin L1 children born and raised in the region who learn German and Italian at school, through exposure within the community and via common media such as radio, the internet and television. Some of these children come from families with a mixed language background, and some of them speak a combination of Ladin, German and/or Italian in the family environment. Individual differences are, of course, to be expected, but what these children share is a combined exposure to the three languages of the community (Ladin, German and Italian) from an early age. The second major subgroup with a completely different set of characteristics is that of first- and second-generation immigrant children who speak a home language that differs from any of the three languages of instruction (Ladin, German and Italian) spoken in the community. These children bring with them their own histories and cultures and, above all, their own linguistic repertoires to the school and to the region. Some of them are born in the area; others outside of the country. As a broad subgroup, however, they typically share the use of a home language that differs from the languages spoken within the community or in the school context.

In addition to the three languages of instruction, being part of the same school means that all children must learn other languages as part of the school curriculum. In most non-English-speaking countries, the study of English as a foreign language is taken up at some point in primary education. In Ladin schools, the study of English begins in fourth year, when children are 10 years old. At this point, Ladin L1 children start studying a fourth language, while immigrant children may start studying or speaking their fifth or sometimes sixth language, depending on the number of languages spoken in the family environment.

In Chapter 3, we will see that minority language speakers who are part of long-established bilingual or multilingual European communities tend to achieve very good results on standardised tests originally designed for monolingual majority language speakers. Evidence of this kind runs counter to the argument reported at the beginning of this section that minority language speakers cannot show their academic knowledge effectively when tested using monolingual tests. In order to devise assessment practices that are suitable, equitable and fair to all students, a first step forward is therefore to gain a better understanding of *who* we are testing, as it is imperative that we are able to describe multilingual speakers in a way that is sufficiently inclusive and reflects the wide variety of multiple language speakers we find in our schools.

2.3.4 The viability of multilingual testing in education

There are two main types of multilingual tests in education: (a) multilingual-by-translation tests and (b) multilingual-by-design tests. Multilingual-by-translation tests are monolingual tests that are fully translated into one or more languages but essentially remain monolingual versions of the original tests. By contrast, multilingual-by-design tests are tests with instructions or content in more than one language and/or scoring criteria that allow for answers in more than one language. Both types of tests have been explored as a possible solution for students with language difficulties in school and have been successful in many educational contexts around the world.

Holistic approaches to testing and assessment often cite this type of evidence in support of the claim that tests for immigrants and minority language speakers should allow students to access and use all their language resources during the assessment process. The literature on multilingual assessment, however, mostly refers to scenarios involving bilingual children and to tests offered in two languages, so what we know about the possible effectiveness of multilingual tests remains somewhat limited to date. While the success of bilingual tests across bilingual educational contexts is very encouraging, extending the practice to the multilingual classroom raises the question of whether the same approach is truly viable when several languages are involved.

If bilingual tests are a feasible option in most educational contexts – for example, in schools with a homogeneous population of bilingual students and teachers – the same cannot be said about multilingual tests and heterogeneous classroom contexts where the administration of a multilingual test could turn out to be a real challenge. If we imagine for a moment the range of students who attend a school located in a multilingual area where two or three languages are regularly spoken within the community, we can immediately grasp the complexity associated with designing, administering and scoring a hypothetical multilingual test. Is the test going to be written using one language and then translated into other languages (multilingual-by-translation test) or is it going to be written using multiple languages and then scored by accepting answers in multiple languages (multilingual-by-design test)? If the latter, which languages will be used? Should these be both the students' home languages and the languages of instruction, or only the latter?

Tests in multiple languages are inevitably more laborious for test writers and teachers and are likely to be highly time-consuming for anyone involved in the process of designing, administering and scoring a test of this kind. Tests may also need to be simplified, i.e. written to ensure they contain less text or simpler text or include more visuals in the form of images, graphs or drawings that can be universally understood. Not all test writers or teachers have developed enough linguistic awareness to be able to simplify a text or make it translatable. Also, teachers may not have the time to provide translations into multiple languages or may lack the necessary skills to translate a test and ensure item equivalence between languages. These are a tiny fraction of the problems that may be encountered when designing multilingual tests for a truly multilingual class. The complexity of these challenges will be elaborated further in Chapter 5, where the stages involved in multilingual test development and the type of obstacles that can be encountered are described in more detail.

The idea of assessing academic content by giving students the opportunity of showing their knowledge in more than one language is not only noble and fair, but it is also logistically difficult and, in some cases, impractical. However, there are ways of designing good quality tests for culturally and linguistically diverse student populations that adhere to the principles of validity, inclusivity, viability and accessibility (VIVA).

Validity is a broad criterion that tells us whether we can make accurate predictions about individuals based on their test scores. Construct validity is one type of validity that refers to the accuracy with which a test is measuring the construct in question. A good quality test must show good construct validity, even in a translated or simplified format, which means that the test must successfully measure all the stated learning objectives by providing versions of similar difficulties in all languages. This applies to all multilingual tests, whether they are multilingual-by-translation or multilingual-by-design tests.

Inclusivity refers to who the assessment is designed for. A test should be designed for linguistically and culturally diverse student populations of learners who may have different levels of proficiency in the language(s) of testing. A test is inclusive when it is designed for the multilingual population in general, not for a subset of the multilingual population such as immigrants or minority language speakers with poor language proficiency in the language(s) of testing.

A good quality test must also show viability, i.e. it must offer a truly workable option. In multilingual tests, viability is one of the most difficult challenges of all, since viability and the number of languages to be included in a test have an inverse relationship with each other, that is, the more languages that must be represented in the test, the lower the viability of the test.

Finally, a good quality test must also show accessibility, i.e. it should be easy to understand for all students, including those with limited proficiency in the language(s) of instruction, and must give students the opportunity to access their knowledge resources to complete the test. These resources can be internal (personal language or content knowledge) or external (use of language support).

While it is important to understand that different types of multilingual tests rarely meet all the VIVA principles to the same extent, these principles can function as a guide for teachers and test developers engaged in designing tests for multilingual populations.

2.4 An Integrated Approach to Multilingual Testing and Assessment

At the beginning of the chapter, I discussed how current discourse on multilingual testing and assessment is polarised at two irreconcilable extremes. On the one hand, traditional approaches support the use of monolingual tests that are typically associated with an 'old' way of testing and are considered insufficiently inclusive for multilingual populations. On the other, holistic approaches argue that they are the 'new', fair and equitable solution in testing and support students' multiple languages becoming part of the assessment process. However, the use of tests written in multiple languages is not viable when several languages are involved, which is why no solution to this problem has been delivered to date. So, how can we move forward?

Designing multilingual tests suitable for populations with very diverse language profiles is a very challenging task because of the number of variables to be considered that cannot be easily accommodated in a single test. Finding a solution that everyone agrees on does not seem to be a realistic objective. Since the perfect solution does not exist, the next best solution is, in my view, a compromise position. I am writing this book in the full awareness that the proposed integrated approach to testing and assessment is a mediating position that may generate both agreement and disagreement among scholars in the field. As both traditional and holistic approaches present their own drawbacks and limitations, my approach proposes to overcome existing barriers by introducing greater flexibility in the way tests are designed, administered, scored and interpreted. Flexibility, however, requires an open mind and a collective willingness to consider alternatives and implement strategies that integrate information of various kinds.

The integrated approach to testing and assessment was conceived in response to the general need to expand the current repertoire of assessment practices for multilingual populations and overcome the obstacles dictated by the traditional/holistic distinction. The approach aims to be a flexible solution that can answer educational questions about students' progress and performance by making use of all relevant and reliable information about the test and the test takers. Central to the approach is the distinction between (1) designing, administering and scoring multilingual tests; and (2) assessing multilingual individuals. The approach rests on the assumption that by combining different types of information, test writers, examiners and educators will be able to make more informed decisions when designing, administering, scoring and interpreting tests for multilingual populations.

This approach, as previously defined, refers to the process of gathering information about the knowledge, skills and abilities of multilingual learners, using tools *designed* for linguistically and culturally diverse populations that may be *administered* in multiple modalities, *scored* by multilingual examiners and *interpreted* using data about the test takers that includes information about their language background and living environment. Its underlying conceptualisation and the relevance of each component will become clearer throughout this volume, which also provides a number of recommendations on developing multilingual tests using the integrated approach to testing and assessment (Chapter 5) and an example of how the approach was used for formative assessment purposes in trilingual education in South Tyrol, Italy (Chapter 7).

3 From Bilingual to Multilingual Education

Most educational contexts around the world have been confronted with the difficulties associated with the need to provide good quality education to linguistically and culturally diverse students who have little or no knowledge of the language(s) of instruction. The issue has been dealt with in different ways, from children being integrated into mainstream education by using various forms of language support to the establishment of bilingual or multilingual education programmes specifically designed for immigrant and/or minority language populations.

Bilingual education is commonly understood to be education delivered in two languages where the two languages are used to teach academic content, such as mathematics, history and geography, and are also regular school subjects. As a result of the rapid spread of English and the growing demand for English language education, many schools running bilingual programmes have extended their activities to English as a third language (L3) and the use of English to teach content has become widespread.

Multilingual education can be broadly defined as a form of education that uses three or more languages to teach academic content and where the amount and extent of language instruction may vary from one programme to another. The number of languages involved adds considerable complexity for the school, as effective teaching requires well-structured pedagogical approaches that teach language and content in a balanced manner.

Most bilingual and multilingual education programmes aim to help students achieve a high level of proficiency in the languages of instruction by the end of the school cycle. This can be a very challenging objective to accomplish when students speak different first languages (L1s) in the home environment. The majority of schools running bilingual and multilingual programmes have a good level of awareness of how to help students learn language, and most of the pedagogical decisions teachers make tend to align with the number of different factors widely known to affect language development, such as the amount and quality of written and oral input, the level of support that both the family and the school need to provide to the learner, the role of students' personal aptitude towards language learning and their motivation to learn a second language (L2). Schools are generally committed to providing a good learning experience for their students and tend to establish a close level of cooperation between teaching staff and the students' families.

The emphasis on academic content and/or language instruction depends on schools' educational goals and priorities, and these can vary substantially from programme to programme. This chapter presents an overview of the major types of bilingual and multilingual education programmes available, placing special emphasis on their aims and objectives and, where possible, their degree of success. Since the concern of this volume is multilingual testing and assessment, which is a field heavily reliant on the bilingual education and bilingual assessment literature, this chapter begins with a brief summary of bilingual education, including when bilingual education started, how it developed and how it eventually paved the way for the introduction of multilingual education programmes in a variety of multilingual contexts. The overview begins with the strong and weak forms of bilingual education that mostly originated in Canada and the United States (Section 3.1), before moving on to content and language integrated learning (CLIL) education in Europe (Section 3.2) and some of the issues related to CLIL and assessment (Section 3.3). This is followed by an overview of multilingual education programmes and their unique association with minority language populations and their specific educational needs (Section 3.4). The question of whether functional multilingualism is an achievable objective is explored in the section that follows by focusing on three entirely different European contexts: Finland, the Basque Country and Italy (Section 3.5). Section 3.6 concludes the chapter with a discussion of one of the most frequently asked questions about immigrant students in education: How long does it take for immigrant children to reach the academic level of their native peers?

3.1 Strong and Weak Forms of Bilingual Education

The beginning of bilingual education programmes is often associated with the 20th century, but this form of education is not a recent phenomenon and has, in fact, been around for at least 5000 years (Baker, 2001). Baker notes that if we do not want to lose sight of the cultural, political and economic reasons that led to the introduction of bilingual programmes in different geographical contexts, it is important to discuss bilingual education without divorcing it from its legitimate historical roots. In countries such as the United States and Canada, and in European countries such as Sweden and England, 'bilingual education must be linked to the historical context of immigration as well as political movements such as civil rights, equality of educational opportunity, affirmative action and melting pot (integrationist, assimilationist) policies' (Baker, 2001: 182). In bilingual areas of Europe such as Ireland and Wales, bilingual programmes are further tied to language rights movements and the rise of nationalism (Baker, 2001; Baker & Wright, 2017).

Several types of bilingual education programmes are available and different types of classifications have been proposed. These classifications are typically based on the status of regional/national languages and the type and number of languages spoken in the home, at school and/or in the community (for reviews, see Baetens Beardsmore, 1993; Baker, 2001; Baker & Wright, 2017; Hurajovà, 2015; Rossell & Baker, 1996). A broad but very useful classification is that of *strong* and *weak* forms of education (Baker, 2001; García, 2009). The distinction between these terms is based on the overall aims of the programmes, the expected language outcome for the students and whether the programmes promote additive or subtractive forms of bilingualism (Lambert, 1975).

The difference between additive and subtractive bilingualism lies in the relationship between the two languages and the possible outcomes associated with the acquisition of the L2. In additive bilingualism, the L2 is acquired without any cost to the L1, which continues to be learned, used and developed in parallel with the L2. L2 learning is not meant to replace the L1 but to add a language to the learner's existing repertoire. This would be the case with French immersion programmes in Canada, for instance, where the teaching of French in anglophone areas does not have a detrimental effect on the acquisition of English as a native language. In contrast, in cases of subtractive bilingualism, the L2 implies a negative impact on the L1, which can be lost or significantly weakened as a result of the L2 learning process. This would be the case for an immigrant child with, for instance, Turkish as his/her L1, who is learning English as an L2 in the UK. The child will eventually lose the L1, or the L1 will show signs of attrition over time.

Weak forms of bilingual education are mostly associated with subtractive bilingualism where the expected outcome is either monolingualism or limited bilingualism. Strong forms of bilingual education are instead associated with additive bilingualism where the expected outcomes are bilingualism and biliteracy. Strong forms of bilingual education are designed for both majority and minority language speakers, while weak forms of education are mostly designed for minority language speakers and immigrants who need to learn the language of instruction and integrate into mainstream education (Baker, 2006).

Within the broad range of bilingual education programmes, many different variants are in use. Among the strong forms of bilingual education, immersion is perhaps the best known. In immersion education, majority language children are fully immersed in the L2 and are taught subjects using the L2. This is the case with immersion programmes in Canada, for instance, where English L1 students in anglophone areas study in French, the other official language of the country. Within immersion programmes, we can also distinguish between early and late programmes, the difference being the age at which the children start attending the programme. Some programmes are also referred to as partial immersion or full immersion programmes, where partial immersion is used to refer to the teaching of only some of the school subjects in the L2, while full immersion refers to the teaching of all subjects in the L2 (see Baker, 2006; Dicks & Genesee, 2017; Swain, 2000). There are also maintenance or heritage programmes whose aims are to maintain the child's L1 in which teaching is typically offered partly in the L1 and partly in the L2, and two-way or dual-language programmes designed for mixed language minority and majority students with academic subjects taught in both languages (Kagan *et al.*, 2017; Lindholm-Leary & Block, 2010; Potowski & Muñoz-Basols, 2018; Vance, 2019).

All these strong forms of education share the common objective of having students achieve bilingualism and biliteracy in the two languages of instruction. In contrast, weak forms of education have monolingualism and limited bilingualism as their main educational outcome (Baker, 2006) and typically include programmes that aim to integrate students into mainstream education and facilitate their transition into a new educational system. Integration is achieved in different ways, from separating students from mainstream classrooms for L2 instruction to offering varying degrees of language support in or after class.

One issue that has often been raised about strong forms of bilingual education concerns their overall effectiveness. While some reviews of bilingual education programmes are available (Baetens Beardsmore, 1993; Baker, 2006; Baker & Wright, 2017; Cummins, 1998; Hurajovà, 2015; Rossell & Baker, 1996), what seems to be missing are systematic and direct comparisons of the overall effectiveness of these programmes. This lack is mainly due to the differences between programmes, which make them virtually incomparable, and the general lack of common and reliable methodological tools for such comparisons. That said, it is now widely accepted that strong forms of bilingual education are the most conducive to language learning and that teaching in two languages has no negative consequences for learning school subjects. In contrast, weak forms of bilingual education seem to be the least effective in helping students develop bilingual language competence and are the least preferred option for bilingual language development (Baker, 2006).

3.2 Content and Language Integrated Learning

The most significant addition to the long list of approaches to bilingual education is the CLIL approach that spread across Europe from the 1990s onwards. The term was originally proposed in the 1990s in Europe, where interest in supporting foreign language education on a large scale motivated the initial discussions associated with the introduction of CLIL in European schools. CLIL is formally defined as 'a dual-focused educational approach in which an additional language is used for the learning and teaching of both content and language' (Coyle et al., 2010: 1). Four basic principles are often used to describe this approach, known as the 4Cs: content, cognition, communication and culture (Coyle, 2008; Mehisto et al., 2008). English is the most studied foreign language in Europe (Eurostat, 2019) and, while the CLIL approach is claimed to be suitable for any language, including foreign, second and minority languages, CLIL is now mostly associated with English-medium instruction (Cenoz et al., 2014; Lasagabaster & Sierra, 2009; Merino & Lasagabaster, 2018).

CLIL proponents have claimed it to be an umbrella term for different forms of bilingual education (see Dalton-Puffer et al., 2014). Scholars working in bilingual communities, however, have questioned whether CLIL can be taken to be the same as the bilingual education programmes reviewed earlier in this chapter and as immersion programmes in particular (Cenoz et al., 2014; Lasagabaster & Sierra, 2009). Both Cenoz et al. (2014) and Lasagabaster and Sierra (2009) provide lucid and convincing analyses of the differences between CLIL and immersion programmes that leave little room for doubt about the existence of essential differences between the aims and overall objectives of these programmes, ranging from students' and teachers' interests, expectations and profiles, to the balance between content and language teaching adopted in the classroom context. Moreover, CLIL was conceived with foreign language education in mind, so it does not make much sense to talk about a CLIL approach using students' native languages, which would be the case in most bilingual and multilingual communities around the world (Rasom, 2010).

3.3 CLIL and Assessment

CLIL is now a widespread approach to foreign language education in Europe (Eurydice, 2006; Merino & Lasagabaster, 2018). Over the last two decades, researchers have devoted considerable attention to the challenges that this approach poses for classroom pedagogy, teacher training, students' learning and teachers' competence in the foreign language (Mehisto et al., 2008). Assessment also presents significant challenges (Hönig, 2010) and remains a controversial area of research (Massler et al., 2014; Otto & Estrada, 2019), particularly in relation to the interplay between language and content (Lo & Fung, 2018).

One major point of criticism relates to the CLIL practice of testing content through the foreign language. Lo and Fung (2018) point out that testing English language learners using an L2 has been extensively criticised in the literature, because language learners cannot be expected to perform as well as native peers using an L2. The awareness that students perform better in the L1 than the L2 highlights the general need to understand the relationship between the linguistic and cognitive demands of a test and the proficiency level required to succeed in it.

In the 1970s, Cummins (1979a, 1981a, 1981b) proposed the Basic Interpersonal Communication Skills/Cognitive Academic Language Proficiency (BICS)/(CALP) distinction to refer to the difference between learning sufficient language to succeed in social communication (BICS) and for academic achievement (CALP). The distinction is often cited, but the threshold between the two levels remains an open question that continues to be investigated, including in the study reported in this volume.

Shaw and Imam (2013) provide some interesting insights into the association between the linguistic demands of a test and the level of proficiency needed to succeed in it. The authors analysed the Cambridge International Certificate of Secondary Education (IGCSE) exam, an international qualification for 14- to 16-year-old students regarded as the equivalent of the General Certificate of Secondary Education (GCSE) exams in the UK. Their study, which focused on the linguistic demands of biology, geography and history IGCSE exams, found that while low scores were generally associated with poor knowledge of content, some questions required more advanced language competence than others. Essay questions, for instance, required more advanced language proficiency to be completed successfully. The study confirmed that students must reach a certain threshold in order to perform effectively, which means that CLIL cannot focus only on the content of the test but must also take into account the students' level of proficiency in the language of testing.

In addition to the problem of testing students using a foreign language, there is also the wider question of whether CLIL students should be assessed on language, content or both, and whether one has priority over the other. Normally, it is understood that content takes priority over language but, since both language and content are equally important in CLIL, some also argue that both should be equally assessed (Massler *et al.*, 2014). Moreover, even when it is content that is being evaluated, teachers still focus on language, introducing an inevitable bias in the assessment process (Hönig, 2010).

Several other questions about CLIL and assessment remain to be answered, ranging from which language should be used in the test (the L1 or the L2) to who should write or administer it, how students' progress can be measured effectively and what type of rubrics teachers should use for scoring. Most of the testing instruments used in CLIL classes are relatively frequent testing tools, such as exams, multiple-choice questions and essay questions (Otto & Estrada, 2019); however, as Shaw and Imam (2013) have shown, some of them impose linguistic demands that go beyond students' ability to perform in a foreign language and their use in CLIL classes should therefore be reassessed. The variety and depth of issues that remain on the CLIL agenda suggest that more research on CLIL assessment is indeed needed before future research can offer clear and workable solutions for both teachers and students. CLIL is a relatively young approach to education and, like any new approach, it will take some time before its true effectiveness is understood and the issues that its use raises can be adequately addressed.

3.4 Multilingual Education

Schools interested in multilingual education have turned to bilingual education to understand what works best and what can be implemented when more than two languages are used for teaching. Years of research and practice in bilingual education have provided a wealth of useful information on best practices, pathways to effectiveness and possible pitfalls.

Adding languages to the curriculum increases the practical and theoretical challenges for both educators and academics, who need to consider a whole new set of variables that may ultimately affect learning outcomes, pedagogical approaches and teacher training activities. Among these challenges, one that features highly is the need to conceive multilingual education from a social as well as an individual perspective. A bilingual immersion programme can be successful in a majority language context, but this may not be the case for a multilingual programme where students attending the programme already speak several languages, often from birth, and hear different languages spoken in the community. The external community context, with its languages and communicative practices, enters the school context and shares its natural space, just as the multilingualism fostered within the school environment shapes, influences and reinforces community practices.

While less widespread than bilingual education, multilingual education is becoming increasingly common in a variety of contexts due to the needs of local communities and the growing demand to add English as a language of instruction to the curriculum. Multilingual programmes are usually found in well-established multilingual communities where these programmes were originally created for bilingual or multilingual local populations. In many of these contexts, immigration is a long-standing phenomenon and many immigrants are now well-integrated into the community and mainstream education. In other contexts, immigration is still a relatively recent phenomenon and schools are faced with the task of accommodating large numbers of first-generation immigrant children who enter the school system with poor knowledge of the languages of instruction that they must master in order to successfully complete the school cycle.

There are several trilingual programmes in Europe and the number of children attending these programmes who speak a home language that differs from the three official languages of instruction is constantly increasing. Most schools running trilingual programmes have had to address the question of how to help these new minorities complete their education, and the project conducted in the Ladin Valleys of South Tyrol discussed in this volume arises from such circumstances. The Ladin school board wanted to understand what educational adjustments were needed to help immigrant children successfully complete the trilingual school cycle and, at the same time, wanted to ensure good quality education continued to be delivered for the well-established minorities living in the area who already have advanced knowledge of the three languages of instruction.

In order to complete the education cycle of Ladin schools of South Tyrol, immigrant children are required to learn the three languages of instruction and reach an acceptable level of academic competence in all of them. Most immigrant students continue to use and maintain one, and at times two, home languages in the family context, which they mainly speak with family members or members of their ethnic community. It is therefore not unusual to meet children as young as 4 or 5 years of age who need to learn and manage four or five languages from an early age, who are thus raised using four (or more) languages during their childhood years.

In Europe, we find several multilingual communities with trilingual education programmes (Beetsma, 2002; Cenoz, 2009; Cenoz *et al.*, 2001; Ytsma, 2001). A detailed inventory of these programmes can be found in the Mercator (2011) report, which reviews each programme and the languages taught in each country, as summarised in Table 3.1. Many programmes show the addition of English as a language of instruction, i.e. as a language used to teach content, while those that do not specifically include English, typically add English as a subject after a few years of teaching.

In addition to the European-based programmes listed in Table 3.1, multilingual education is also available in other parts of the world through local education or international schools. To mention a few of these, we have examples of multilingual programmes or advanced discussion about their implementation from many international locations such as China (Adamson & Feng, 2014; Wang & Kirkpatrick, 2019), the United States and South America (Henn-Reinke, 2012) and South Africa (Heugh, 2011). Multilingual education is undoubtedly becoming more common and increasingly accessible, but it is crucial to remember that it is a relatively recent form of education whose assessment practices are inconsistent and do not follow a common trajectory. Each country evaluates programme effectiveness and students' performance in a different way, and the broad range of practices suggests we are still far from reaching any kind of theoretical cohesion.

Table 3.1 Trilingual education in Europe by location and languages of instruction

Location	Languages of instruction
Aosta Valley	French, Italian, English – or German in Walser communities
Aran Valley	Occitan, Catalan, Spanish
Balearic Islands	Catalan, Spanish, English
Basque Country	Basque, Spanish, English
Catalonia	Catalan, Spanish, English
Finland	Finnish, Swedish, English – or German and French
Friesland	Fryslan, Dutch, English
Ladin Valleys	Ladin, German, Italian
Luxembourg	French, German, Luxembourgish
North Frisia	Frisian, Danish, High German
Southern part of Carinthia	German, Slovene, English
Valencian communities	Valencian, Spanish, English

Source: Mercator (2011).

3.5 Is Functional Multilingualism an Achievable Objective?

Multilingual education programmes have a long history in Europe due to the official bilingual status of many countries and the presence of numerous bilingual and multilingual communities scattered around the continent. The evaluation of these programmes has never been comparative in nature as each country has traditionally adopted different methods of evaluation to suit local needs and legal requirements. Despite the differences, however, this section will show that even though different approaches are used to evaluate students' achievements, conclusions are remarkably similar across contexts. This is illustrated by focusing on three sample European locations with completely different histories and cultures: Finland, the Basque Country and Italy.

3.5.1 Finland

Finland is a Nordic country with a population of 5.5 million inhabitants. According to Statistics Finland (n.d.), in 2018, Finnish L1 speakers composed 87.6% of the population, Swedish L1 speakers, 5.2% and speakers of other languages, 7.1%. In 2012, the largest groups of foreign language speakers were the Russian (62,554) and the Estonian (38,364) communities. Over half a million residents of Finland are foreign language speakers (Annual Report on Immigration, 2012). Even though most of the population speaks Finnish as a native language, Finnish and Swedish have equal status within the country and Finland has been officially bilingual by law since 1922 (Latomaa & Nuolijärvi, 2005). In addition to Finnish, Swedish and the immigrant languages, there are also Sami language speakers who live in the northernmost areas of the country (Lapland). Sami languages are those spoken by the indigenous population (Svonni, 2001).

Finland is one of a number of countries that participate in the Programme for International Student Assessment (PISA), an international standardised test that aims to assess the skills and knowledge of 15-year-old children worldwide, focusing on reading, mathematics and science. For a number of years, the Finnish educational system was in the spotlight due to its excellent results in the PISA test (Kupiainen *et al.*, 2009) and, even though results have begun to decline in recent years, sparking a substantial controversy in the Finnish media (Rautalin, 2018), the PISA 2018 results continue to show that Finland has a strong education system, with Finnish students scoring higher than the Organisation for Economic Cooperation and Development (OECD) average in reading, mathematics and science.

The first Finnish and Swedish immersion programme was established in 1987 in the city of Vaasa/Vasa, on the west coast of Finland. This location was chosen because of the high percentage of Swedish speakers living in the area, estimated at the time to be about 25% of the local population. In addition to Swedish and Finnish, immersion schools also introduced additional languages such as English, German and French, with the aim of students achieving functional multilingualism in three or more languages, defined as 'a competence level at which immersion students can act and participate naturally in the daily use of the multiple languages, in line with their age and levels' (Mercator, 2011: 19).

Researchers at the University of Vaasa have been monitoring and evaluating Finnish/Swedish immersion programmes since their implementation, using a comparative approach and focusing on students' performance in the L1 and L2. Immersion and non-immersion students have been compared using national reading tests administered in Grade 3, which are designed to measure language awareness and reading skills. A second form of evaluation has been the national matriculation exam administered 2–4 years after completion of the immersion programme (Mercator, 2011). From the outset, since results were found to be extremely encouraging, a number of other immersion programmes were also established across the country (Björklund, 1997; Björklund & Lasagabaster, 2002; Björklund *et al.*, 2014). In terms of language proficiency, no major differences were found between immersion and non-immersion students for the Finnish L1, while students in immersion programmes were found to be well above those in mainstream education for knowledge of Swedish as an L2. Immersion students also showed a higher level of performance in the English L3 and the German fourth language (L4) (Mercator, 2011).

Taken as a whole, the information from multilingual programmes in Finland indicates that multilingual education is effective and functional multilingualism is an achievable objective. Most importantly, the data shows that immersion programmes have advantages for language learning (higher language competence in the L2 and in additional languages) and no clear disadvantages for the native language (similar competence in the Finnish L1).

3.5.2 The Basque Country

The Basque Country is a multilingual region located between Northern Spain and France. Basque speakers are divided into three main political areas: the Basque Autonomous Community (BAC) and Navarre (both in Spain); and the Pyrenees Department in France. In 2019, the Basque Country had a population of 2,188,017 inhabitants, 7.6% of whom were foreign nationals (Instituto Vasco de Estadística, n.d.). Established in 1979 by the Basque Statute of Autonomy, the BAC includes the provinces of Araba, Bizkaia and Gipuzkoa (Lasagabaster, 2001). Bilingualism in the region is not as widespread as one might expect: 27% of the population older than 16 are bilingual (Spanish/Basque or Spanish/French) and 14.7% are passive bilingual, while 58.3% are Spanish or French monolingual (Encuesta Sociolinguistica, 2011).

The teaching of Basque was banned during Franco's regime (1939–1975), which explains the low number of Basque speakers in the region. This started to change with the 1982 Basic Law on the Standardisation of Basque (Lasagabaster, 2001), when both Basque and Spanish became compulsory school subjects. Three teaching models were introduced, known as Model A (Spanish-medium schools), Model B (mixed Basque and Spanish schools) and Model D (Basque-medium schools). There is no Model C as C is not a letter in the Basque alphabet.

Model A schools are Spanish-medium schools intended for Spanish majority speakers. In these schools, all subjects are taught in Spanish, while Basque is taught as an L2 for 3–5 hours a week. Model B schools are mixed schools where subjects are taught in both Spanish and Basque, with about 50% of the time devoted to each language. Model D schools are Basque-medium schools where subjects are taught in Basque, while Spanish is taught for 3–5 hours a week. These schools were initially conceived as Basque language maintenance programmes, but over the years Spanish majority speakers started to attend them more regularly, making Model D schools immersion programmes as well as maintenance programmes. English is also taught as a school subject in all these schools, and the teaching of English has been met with a very strong level of support from students' families (Cenoz, 2009; Etxeberria & Elosegi, 2008; Lasagabaster, 2000a, 2000b, 2001; Mercator, 2011; Sierra, 2008).

The Basque Country has conducted several studies on its educational programmes (Sierra, 2008). In terms of language competence, research consistently indicates that students attending Spanish-medium schools (Model A) achieve the lowest level of proficiency in Basque, while students in mixed schools (Model B) achieve good competence in Basque but not as high as that of students attending Basque-medium schools (Model D) (Lasagabaster, 2001). An important mark of academic achievement is taken to be the percentage of students who pass the *Selectivitad* exam, a university entrance exam which is compulsory for all students who wish to enter third-level education in Spain. In 2009, the percentage of students passing the test from the BAC was very high, totalling 94.6% of those who took the test in Basque and 89.6% of those who took the test in Spanish (Mercator, 2011). Similarly to the Finnish situation discussed in Section 3.5.1, the information available from the Basque Country thus suggests that the existing multilingual programmes are effective and that functional multilingualism is an achievable objective for students attending these programmes.

3.5.3 Italy

Italy is organised into 15 regions with ordinary status and 5 regions with special autonomous status granted by the constitution to protect local cultures and minority language speakers. The five autonomous regions are Friuli-Venezia Giulia, Sardinia, Sicily, Trentino-Alto Adige/Sudtirol and Valle d'Aosta/Vallée d'Aoste. In these five regions, several minority languages are spoken in addition to the Italian national language. Minority languages are taught in school as subjects and are also used to teach content. Each region has its own history and languages, and this section considers the educational context of two of these regions: Valle d'Aosta/Vallée d'Aoste and Trentino-Alto Adige/Sudtirol.

Valle d'Aosta/Vallée d'Aoste

Valle d'Aosta/Vallée d'Aoste is a region located in the northern part of Italy, bordering Switzerland and France. According to Regione Autonoma Valle d'Aosta (n.d.), in 2018 Valle d'Aosta/Vallée d'Aoste had a population of 126,202, of which 8,294 were of immigrant origin. The largest immigrant groups are from Romania (29.8%), Morocco (18.7%) and Albania (8.9%). The region has three official languages: Italian, French and German. Italian is the language spoken most widely, followed by French and German. Local languages include the Franco-Provençal regional languages and the German Walser dialects spoken in the Lys Valley. Schools in the region devote the same number of hours to the teaching of Italian and French from elementary to secondary school level, and each language is also used to teach content up to the age of 14 (50% in each language), while the amount of exposure begins to vary once students start the secondary school cycle.

Standard German (*Hochdeutsch*) is taught as an L3 in the Walser-speaking context (Lys Valley) and it is also offered as a foreign language in some secondary schools across the region, along with Russian and Spanish. English is taught as a foreign language throughout the region and it is used to teach subjects such as science and technology, as in the rest of the country. In primary schools, the integrated use of the three languages is also widespread for non-language disciplines (Vernetto, 2019). In this complex linguistic setting, local schools are evaluated using two main standardised tests: the National Institute for the Evaluation of the Education and Training System (INVALSI) test (Italian, maths and English) and the PISA test. In recent years, regional law 18/2016 also introduced regional language tests for French, German and English.

The Italian and maths INVALSI tests indicate that at 14 years of age, students' performance is in line with that of students attending schools in the north-west of the country. In regional language tests, 78% of 14-year-old students reach the Common European Framework of Reference for Languages (CEFR) A2+ level in oral comprehension and 55.7% reach the same level in reading comprehension and written production. The INVALSI test in English also shows good results in line with the north-west of the country. Most students reach the A2 level (80%) in reading and 70% in oral skills (SREV, 2019). The PISA test is normally administered in Italian; however, in 2009, the test was administered to 752 students attending secondary schools using Italian or French (SREV, 2010). In line with results from Finland and the Basque Country, these evaluations collectively showed that the education system functions well and, most importantly, overall results did not suggest that the multilingual school system is placing students at any significant disadvantage, particularly for language learning.

Trentino-Alto Adige/Südtirol

Trentino-Alto Adige/Südtirol is an autonomous region located in the northern part of Italy that borders Austria and Switzerland. It is organised into two provinces: the Province of Bolzano-Bozen (Alto Adige/Südtirol) and the Province of Trento (Trentino). According to the latest census in 2011, the Province of Bolzano-Bozen had 504,643 inhabitants (ASTAT, n.d.) with the following native languages: Italian (26.06%), German (69.41%) and Ladin (4.53%). The German spoken in the area is a South Tyrolean dialect. More information about the history of South Tyrol and the school system can be found in Chapter 7.

Three distinct school boards oversee education in the Province of Bolzano-Bozen: the Italian school board, the German school board and the Ladin school board. Article 19 of the 1972 Statute of Autonomy gives all citizens in the area the right to be educated in their mother tongue, and this led to the establishment of different educational models within the region. Italian and German schools teach all subjects in students' native languages (Italian or German) and teach the other language as an

L2. The Ladin school board was given the possibility of introducing a multilingual model which provides a balance between the two teaching languages (German and Italian) and also uses Ladin for communication. Students are expected to reach equal competence in Italian and German throughout the school cycle. The majority of students attending Ladin schools are Ladin L1 speakers, so the model is additionally designed to protect and support the development of the Ladin language and culture and help students maintain Ladin or achieve a good level of proficiency in Ladin through their education. Primary schools place major emphasis on trilingual literacy in German, Italian and Ladin. Lessons are mostly held 1 week in German and 1 week in Italian, while two weekly units are devoted to the Ladin language and culture. Ladin is also used for explanations and general support, while religion is taught in the three languages. In fourth year, English is added as an additional subject (2 hours per week). In secondary education (from the age of 11), half the school subjects are taught in Italian and the other half in German. Maths, for instance, is no longer taught 1 week in Italian and 1 week in German but taught only in German for the entire cycle, while Ladin continues to be used as the language of communication. Such a complex educational system requires staff with substantial language competences and teachers working in Ladin schools are required to pass a trilingualism exam.

All schools in the Province of Bolzano-Bolzen are under a legal obligation to administer the INVALSI national standardised test in local schools (law DPR 80/2013); external evaluations are also legally possible (Provincial law n. 5, 2008, art. 1 bis). Like most other educational systems in Europe, Ladin schools rely on standardised tests to measure overall programme effectiveness, and the results obtained so far have been highly encouraging. According to the PISA 2015 test, 15-year-old students are above the OECD average in financial literacy and are also ranked above the Italian national average. In reading literacy, they are in line with the OECD average and above the Italian national average. The PISA 2018 results also indicate that Ladin students are above the OECD average and the national Italian average in reading, science and maths, while the INVALSI 2018 standardised national test confirms students' strengths in maths and English with scores above the national average. With regard to Italian, students living in areas where German is widely spoken within the community were found to be below the national average, while results remained above the national average in areas where Italian is more widespread. The situation in South Tyrol thus seems to confirm the general effectiveness of the multilingual education system in place and shows that functional multilingualism is an achievable objective that does not place students at any significant disadvantage. Interestingly, the only results below the national average relate to Italian in areas densely populated by German speakers, which confirms the claim that standardised test results must be examined in conjunction with community language information to provide a fair assessment of the situation (De Angelis, 2014). The role of languages spoken within the community is also emphasised in the integrated approach to testing and assessment presented in this volume.

3.5.4 Common features and the unique role of the social context

The languages spoken within the community occupy a prominent place in the integrated approach to testing and assessment because contextual differences can greatly influence how people learn language and how quickly and well they respond to education. Of concern in this volume is that the same test scores can provide very different information when contextual differences are taken into account (De Angelis, 2014). Several contextual differences are associated with multilingual education and affect the evaluation of its programmes. The choice of each country as to which type of evaluation is best suited to the local context is based on local community knowledge, the history of the region and the history of ethnically based social tensions within each region. Moreover, contextual information cannot be divorced from evaluation practices, as it was the social context that provided the motivation – and in some cases the legal obligation – to establish multilingual programmes in the first place.

Differences between countries are expected to exist, and what makes sense in one context may not necessarily make sense in another. The three teaching models implemented in the Basque Country (Models A, B and D), for instance, would not make much sense in Finland or Italy, where local communities came to share the same living environment following an entirely different sequence of historical events. Local community knowledge is also deeply connected with local politics. Let us not forget that not so long ago in areas such as the Basque Country (Spain) or Alto Adige/Südtirol (Italy), people lost their lives due to internal ethnically-based conflicts, and government officials and politicians may still feel compelled to act in a specific direction due to past events that left a long trail of friction, antagonism and pain.

Each multilingual programme approaches the task of teaching language and academic content in different ways, adopting pedagogical strategies that make sense for the local context, and teachers are usually local people trained to understand and foster local community language practices. They learn to be effective in their unique educational environment thanks to a combination of pre-service and in-service teacher training, personal experience, community knowledge and language knowledge. Driven by the desire to protect the languages spoken within the local community, researchers and educators are deeply motivated to understand how effective local multilingual programmes are in comparison to mainstream education programmes. This within-country comparative approach that can be observed in most places is therefore understandable and reasonable, although arguably improvable as it is based on standardised tests that are not sufficiently refined to be able to capture contextual differences found in bilingual and multilingual environments.

Even though programme evaluation practices differ from country to country, some common features can be observed. A first feature that most countries share is the extensive use of standardised tests for evaluation purposes, hence the need for the testing industry to consider how to integrate multilinguals' language background and the languages spoken in the community in the testing process. Every country needs to evaluate its own educational system to ensure that the overall quality of education remains high and consistent in all areas, which includes identifying underperforming students and possible areas of weakness within the system that may benefit from targeted intervention. While the use of standardised tests in education has been strongly criticised in the literature (Doecke *et al.*, 2010; Menken, 2008; Shen & Cooley, 2008; Zwick *et al.*, 2008), standardised tests continue to play an essential role in assessing quality in education, and tests are frequently a legal requirement with which schools are required to comply. Notwithstanding their limitations, standardised tests are also regularly used for multilingual assessment purposes because they provide publicly available and therefore readily usable data without the need for additional data collection that can be costly and time-consuming. This is connected to the second trait that most multilingual educational systems seem to share, namely the interest they show in demonstrating that multilingual programmes are effective for teaching both language and content. Frequent comparisons with mainstream education programmes suggest a general need to strengthen public opinion concerning the effectiveness of these programmes and to show that students studying and learning several languages at the same time are not going to be disadvantaged in any way.

A further common characteristic is that multilingual programmes are effective in most locations and seem to offer significant language advantages to students. Knowledge of the L1 does not appear to be negatively affected by exposure to additional languages, while students generally show significant advantages in foreign or L2 learning, including English. In some cases, standardised test scores also show some disadvantages for immigrant students or long-standing minority language speakers, and when results of this kind occur in multilingual contexts, they are often difficult to interpret because standardised tests do not take local community information into account.

The importance of analysing standardised test results in conjunction with community language information was shown in De Angelis (2014). The author reanalysed standardised test data for the Italian school board of South Tyrol, Italy, showing how the same set of results can provide very different information once read in conjunction with local language information. The comparison highlighted the connection between lower test results in the Italian test and students' place of residence. Those who lived in German-speaking areas had far fewer opportunities to use Italian in their daily lives than those in Italian-speaking areas, and the different amount of exposure was clearly reflected in the lower test scores in the Italian test. On the whole, the study showed the danger of pooling data from students living in areas where different languages are used in the community, as doing so can lead to significant misinterpretation of the data and, as a result, to unnecessary remedial actions and probably unnecessary costs. The results of the INVALSI 2018 test for Ladin schools in South Tyrol further confirmed the effect of community language practices on test scores, as children attending schools in German-speaking areas scored below national standards in the Italian test, probably due to low exposure to Italian in their daily lives.

Even though it has often been claimed that the use of standardised tests is unfair to immigrant and minority language speakers because students tend to underperform in a language that is not their mother tongue (De Backer *et al.*, 2017; Gorter & Cenoz, 2017; Shohamy, 2011; Shohamy & Menken, 2015), it should also be noted that many minority language speakers in multilingual education would not perform well in the L1 because they are regularly taught in non-dominant languages. The testing industry seems to have made very little effort to integrate information about local community contexts and students' language profiles into the assessment process, even though the information is easy to obtain and can be used to analyse test scores on multiple levels so that comparisons are fairer, more equitable and, above all, more accurate for all concerned. Some have explicitly argued that the testing industry is not interested in abandoning traditional monolingual tests (Dendrinos, 2019). The more evidence that is provided as to why multilinguals should not be compared to monolinguals and how the testing industry can adapt to new criteria, the more likely it is that the needs of multilinguals will be met.

3.6 How Long Does it Take for Immigrant Children to Reach the Academic Level of Their Native Peers?

Most of the multilingual programmes available in Europe and other parts of the world were initially established for the education of children from bilingual and multilingual local communities. With increasing migration, however, immigrant children have also begun to enrol in these programmes, bringing their mother tongues with them, adding a considerable layer of complexity for schools.

Multilingual programmes have gradually come under the spotlight because of the growing number of immigrant children attending these programmes. Immigrant children have native languages that differ from the languages of instruction, which poses considerable pedagogical challenges for teachers who may need to introduce school languages in stages and not always simultaneously. In the Ladin Valleys of South Tyrol, Italy, many immigrant children as young as 5 or 6 years of age are learning to manage three languages of instruction (Ladin, Italian and German) while maintaining the home language in the family environment. This can be a significant challenge for the school, the children and the families. From the schools' perspective, these children have language profiles that do not match those of the local student population, which entails that policies and practices must adapt to this difference in order to deliver successful education.

The presence of different student populations raises further questions in relation to testing and assessment. In Section 3.5, we have seen that students who attend multilingual programmes generally do well and tend to achieve better results than those attending mainstream education, particularly in language learning. While this information is reassuring, it also raises some broader questions about what current assessment practices can tell us about students' progress in multilingual education. The findings, which are mostly based on nationwide standardised testing, seem to conflict with the general view that multilingual assessment should *not* rely on tests devised for monolingual populations, as monolingual tests will inevitably place multilinguals at a disadvantage (De Backer *et al.*, 2017; Gonzalez, 2012; Gorter & Cenoz, 2017; Shohamy, 2011; Shohamy & Menken, 2015). As we have seen, most multilingual students attending multilingual programmes do not seem to be placed at any disadvantage, which leads us to reconsider the question of who we are testing and the extent to which pooling students with different language profiles affects test consistency and reliability.

Students attending multilingual programmes are not a uniform population. Most multilingual communities have a mix of long-established minorities, second-generation immigrants and newly arrived first-generation immigrants, so the following core groups can be identified: (a) recently arrived first-generation immigrants with little or no knowledge of the language of instruction and a home language that typically differs from the languages of instruction; (b) second-generation immigrants with a home language that differs from the languages of instruction; and (c) local multilinguals with variable exposure to the languages of instruction.

One of the most frequently asked questions by school boards and ministries of education in relation to the immigrant population is: How long does it take for immigrant children to reach the academic level of their native peers? An answer to this question is not as straightforward as it may seem, because the estimated time of learning depends on a number of different factors, such as the level of literacy already achieved in the L1, the sociolinguistic environment in which the immigrant lives, the quality and quantity of exposure to the languages of instruction, the number and type of languages spoken within the community, the number and type of background languages already known and the patterns of language use in the home environment (for further discussions, see Herzog-Punzenberger et al., 2017).

Some of the most influential studies on immigrants' speed of language development can be traced back to the 1970s and the work of Cummins (1979a, 1979b, 1981a, 1981b, 2008), who introduced the well-known distinction between BICS and CALP to highlight the difference between learning enough language for effective social communication and for success in the school context. BICS is used to refer to the basic language that minority language speakers need to communicate with others. This basic level is usually achieved fairly quickly, within an average of 2 years of arrival. By contrast, CALP is used to refer to the level of language that is required to succeed in the school context. The student needs to understand and express ideas and notions to varying degrees of complexity, for which basic knowledge of the language of instruction is not enough. CALP is more cognitively demanding and the level of development required for efficient speaking, reading, writing and listening is more advanced.

Cummins (1979a, 1979b, 1981a, 1981b) introduced the distinction between BICS and CALP when he realised that many teachers in Canada were directing minority language speakers to special needs assessment services whenever they believed the children had already acquired enough language to succeed in school. However, the truth of the matter was that many of those children had only acquired sufficient language to engage in successful social communication but had not reached a level that allowed them to engage effectively with academic material; in other words, they were not linguistically ready to succeed in education. These early findings are linked to a study on psychological reports and referral forms submitted by more than 400 teachers working in Canada who requested special needs assessment services (Cummins, 1980, 1984). Upon analysing the data, Cummins found that when the children had mastered enough language for social communication, both teachers and psychologists regarded them as proficient in English and therefore as fully capable of functioning at the required level in the school context. The same children, however, were continuing to underperform at school and were also displaying poor performance in psychological assessment tests involving verbal and cognitive measures. Performance data was therefore in stark contrast with teachers' and psychologists' beliefs about what these immigrant children were capable of doing with the host language. The consequences of not distinguishing between what are now known as BICS and CALP were considerable, as many of these children were being identified as having disabilities they did not have and were being assigned to special education programmes they did not need. To some extent, this is still happening today, particularly in countries with recent immigration.

The patterns Cummins (1981b) had identified were subsequently confirmed using additional data made available by the Toronto board of education. The additional data analysis focused on identifying the time taken by immigrant students to develop academic language proficiency that could be considered comparable to that of native peers, the results of which clearly showed that minority language speakers needed an average of 5–7 years to reach comparable levels of language proficiency.

The average gap between the time it took minority language speakers to develop BICS (1–2 years) and CALP (5–7 years) was later confirmed by several other studies investigating similar questions (Hakuta et al., 2000; Levin & Shohamy, 2008; Mori & Calder, 2013; Shohamy, 2011; Thomas & Collier, 2002). From these studies, literacy emerges as a particularly important component, as it takes an average of 5–7 years for learners with L1 literacy to catch up with native peers and an average of 7–9 years for children to do the same if they have no previous schooling or literacy in the L1.

Further insights come from a large-scale study of 299 schools and a total of 2761 students in Israel (Levin & Shohamy, 2008; Shohamy, 2011). This study compared the performance of two groups of immigrants in mathematics and language (Hebrew), one from the former USSR and the other from Ethiopia. The children who participated in the study were in Grades 5, 9 and 11, and a monolingual control group was also used. The study found that, for both subjects and depending on age and group, it took between 5 and 11 years for these immigrant children to reach the level of their native peers, i.e. a slightly longer period than the one Cummins had originally identified. It was also found that some Ethiopians never managed to reach their native peers' language standard and were thus unable to close the gap on Israeli Hebrew monolinguals.

Several years later, Shohamy (2011) questioned whether testing all students in Hebrew was the best way for them to answer a question about timing and learning. In hindsight, she wondered where things could have been done differently and argued that the use of monolingual testing with immigrant populations may not have been the best approach after all, because the use of Hebrew placed minority language speakers at a significant disadvantage. She also questioned whether it is even legitimate for us to ask how long it takes immigrant children to reach the level of native peers, since we already know that immigrant children have weaker language skills and cannot perform as well as native speakers.

In most contexts, immigrant children attend transitional programmes or are provided with language support that helps them learn the language of instruction and transition more easily to mainstream education. Thomas and Collier (2002) published a well-known report on research conducted in the United States, titled 'A National Study of School Effectiveness for Language Minority Students' Long-Term Academic Achievement'. The report provides detailed information about the level of achievement found over a 5-year period (1996–2001) in different types of school programmes in the United States, set up to offer K-12 teaching to linguistically diverse student populations. Among those examined were transitional programmes which normally provide instruction for short periods of time, from 1 to 3 years. Thomas and Collier (2002) do not recommend that children with no proficiency in the language of instruction are placed in these programmes, as longitudinal data shows that it takes a minimum of 4 years for children to develop sufficient proficiency in the L2, provided they have received at least 4 years of formal education in the home country. According to the authors, a core predictor of school success is the amount of education already received in the L1.

The importance of L1 education had already been identified in the early 1980s by Cummins (1979, 1981a, 1981b), who proposed two other influential hypotheses: the 'Developmental Interdependence Hypothesis' and the 'Threshold Hypothesis'. The Developmental Interdependence Hypothesis posits that the positive effects of bilingualism emerge only when competence in the L1 has been suitably developed, while the Threshold Hypothesis sets additional boundaries by proposing that 'there may be threshold levels of linguistic competence which a bilingual child must attain both in order to avoid cognitive disadvantages and allow the potentially beneficial aspects of bilingualism to influence his cognitive and academic functioning' (Cummins, 1979: 222).

The identification of potential threshold levels is further examined in the study reported in this volume, so I do not go into more detail in this section. At present, however, it should be remembered that immigrant children develop their languages at different speeds, depending on the amount of exposure to oral input and the support they receive from the school and the family. Fundamental to this process are personal aptitude and motivation, as well as the opportunity to communicate with others living within the same community (De Angelis, 2012). The languages spoken within the community and the children's personal language background remain two crucial factors for both learning and assessment, and several researchers have already examined their role with students of different profiles living in different contexts. The outcome of this work is reviewed in Chapter 4, which discusses the type of multilingual assessment practices that were previously used in education that focused either on designing multilingual tests or on grouping test takers according to language background.

4 Multilingual Assessment Practices in Education

The monolingual construct has dominated the field of testing and assessment for a very long time, but our understanding of language learning and language development has also grown considerably in recent decades, and this construct now seems to be in sharp contrast to everything we know about multilingual competence and how multilinguals communicate in real life (Shohamy, 2011). This limitation has motivated many researchers to work towards improving current assessment practices and explore alternative options, such as focusing on how to make tests more suitable for linguistically and culturally diverse student populations or grouping students according to their language background and living environment. This chapter examines this type of research with the aim of presenting an overview of the different types of contributions made over the years. It begins by considering the (negative) implications of monolingual testing for students, teachers and test developers (Section 4.1), before moving on to discuss research that has focused on how to improve tests (Section 4.2) and the advantages of grouping students according to language background and/or languages spoken within the community (Section 4.3).

4.1 Monolingual Testing: Implications for Students, Teachers and Test Developers

It has been repeatedly claimed that the use of monolingual tests in education discriminates against immigrants and minority language speakers and has been shown to provide unreliable and biased test results. Most of the objections highlight the disadvantages of using monolingual tests, which range from their excessive difficulty for students who do not have the necessary language skills to succeed in the test to undue referrals of healthy children to special needs services. Monolingual tests are also argued to be unfair to teachers and test developers who may not be fully familiar with the difficulties that multilinguals are likely to encounter when completing a test in a non-dominant language.

To begin with the proficiency-based arguments, three core objections can be distinguished in the literature. The first objection is based on the fact that monolingual tests assume that all students can achieve native-like competence in all their languages (López *et al.*, 2016; Shohamy, 2011; Stavans & Hoffmann, 2015). This assumption is, however, untenable, since people who speak several languages do not normally achieve the same level of competence – and, above all, multiple L1-like competences – in all their languages. Long before, Grosjean (1985, 1992) had already argued that bilinguals are not the sum of two monolinguals in one person to express the idea that an individual is not the sum of several monolingual competences. The same principle applies to multilingual individuals, who cannot be considered to be the sum of several monolinguals in one person. Multilinguals are individuals with unique linguistic and cognitive profiles who have their own strengths and weaknesses but who can also emerge as poor students when directly compared to their monolingual peers.

The second objection relates to taking native-like competence as the main performance benchmark in testing. Setting a monolingual standard entails that most minority language speakers and immigrant students will not be able to perform to their full potential due to a lack of the necessary language knowledge to succeed in the test (Escamilla *et al.*, 2003, 2014, 2018; García, 2009; Gandara & Randall, 2019; Gorter & Cenoz, 2017; Hopewell & Escamilla, 2014; López *et al.*, 2016; Shohamy, 2011; Wright & Li, 2008). Students may be unable to answer because they do not fully understand the test questions or may lack the necessary language skills to provide answers that are sufficiently clear or elaborate. When these students are tested in a non-dominant language, language gaps inevitably arise, placing them at a great disadvantage (De Backer *et al.*, 2017; Gorter & Cenoz, 2017; Shohamy & Menken, 2015).

The third objection is connected to the general expectation that students will answer the test questions using the language of testing, even though they may be familiar with other languages and may give a better answer if allowed to answer in full or partly in the dominant language (López *et al.*, 2016, 2017; Shohamy, 2011; Shohamy & Menken, 2015; Sierens & Van Avermaet, 2014). Multilingual speakers who cannot remember a word in one language tend to show what they know by drawing on other language sources that are available to them. Language mixing is a very common occurrence, and marking words in other languages as errors, or ignoring students' expressive attempts altogether, can have a negative impact on their perceptions of the value of language and, in the immediate term, on overall test results. Multilingual students who are not given the opportunity to express themselves using all the resources available to them end up being penalised for lack of language knowledge rather than lack of content knowledge.

With regard to the impact of monolingual testing on healthcare, monolingual tests have been repeatedly associated with the referral of healthy bilingual children to special needs services they do not need

(Cummins, 1980, 1984; Rhodes *et al.*, 2005; Sanchez *et al.*, 2013). It is often confusing for teachers to draw a line between genuine developmental language delays and delays due to typical second language (L2) development. Teachers are usually the first to raise concerns about potential developmental delays with the school or the students' families, hence the need for them to be adequately trained to understand normal patterns of language development and how long it takes for a child to develop the ability to communicate socially and academically in an L2. Although Cummins' pioneering work in this area has greatly contributed to raising awareness that not all delays reflect an underlying medical condition, the problem continues to emerge on a regular basis and remains largely unresolved (Armon-Lotem *et al.*, 2015; Meschi *et al.*, 2012; Samson & Lesaux, 2009).

The unfairness linked to monolingual testing concerns not only students but also test developers and teachers who may not be fully familiar with the type of problems immigrant and minority language students encounter when trying to interpret or answer questions in a language they have not fully mastered (Martiniello, 2008). While most teachers would know how to simplify test content or test instructions for assessment purposes, not everyone would be able to do so without explicit training. Test developers, in particular, may have undergone subject-specific training but be totally oblivious to the effects of linguistic demands on non-native speakers' test performance, i.e. they may lack the required metalinguistic awareness for a competent intervention and the necessary understanding of the process of text simplification to introduce changes that are meaningful and effective.

What teachers and test developers support in testing may also affect students' perceptions of what is expected of them in education and even the way they respond to a test item. Test developers and teachers make several language decisions in their work, from choosing the language(s) of testing to deciding to use monolingual or multilingual rubrics for scoring, and these decisions typically penalise the use of languages other than the language of testing during the scoring process. As such, these language decisions can have a profound impact on students' beliefs about testing (Gandara & Randall, 2019). For example, students may feel it is unacceptable to answer questions using more than one language or, when writing essays, may feel the need to be extra vigilant in not using rhetorical styles that belong to a different linguistic and cultural tradition.

Overall, the variety of objections to the use of monolingual tests with immigrant and minority language speakers has greatly contributed to raising awareness among teachers, educators and test developers of the range of problems students encounter when taking a test in a non-dominant language. These objections, however, are not in themselves sufficient to solve the problems identified; they only highlight the need for a solution which, in the context of multilingual testing and assessment, must be easy to use in the classroom. Section 4.2 presents a summary of the kinds of adaptations to tests that have been explored up to now and highlights the most promising efforts in improving the assessment process.

4.2 Focusing on Tests

Several scholars have focused their efforts on how to improve the way tests are designed, administered and scored so that they can be more suitable for linguistically and culturally diverse student populations. These efforts include the use of bilingual and multilingual scoring rubrics (Section 4.2.1), the introduction of bilingual test instructions with the option of answering test questions in multiple languages (Section 4.2.2) and test accommodations such as simplification, translation and providing tests in the students' L1 (Section 4.2.3). Examples of research in each category are discussed.

4.2.1 Bilingual and multilingual scoring rubrics

Scoring rubrics are valuable tools to achieve consistency in grading and can be used for a range of purposes, from programme evaluation to classroom assessment (Stevens & Levi, 2013). Rubrics are defined as 'descriptive scoring systems that allow observers to assign a numeric value to a piece of work or a performance' (Salkind, 2010: 1291).

Research on the effectiveness of bilingual scoring rubrics has been particularly active in the US context, where several scholars have been working on literacy models for bilinguals. One of the best-known models is the Literacy Squared in Action model, a biliteracy model designed to develop literacy skills in emerging English–Spanish bilinguals (Escamilla et al., 2003, 2014, 2018; Hopewell & Escamilla, 2014; Soltero-González et al., 2016). The Literacy Squared project started in 2004 and went through several phases of implementation. During the first phase, researchers worked with a total of 19 schools across two different states. The second phase involved a more in-depth study of three Colorado schools, and in the third phase the project was extended to a total of 5000 children and 250 teachers (Escamilla et al., 2018).

The Literacy Squared model assesses emerging bilinguals holistically using the Literacy Squared writing rubric for both Spanish and English, in whose use teachers are trained. The novelty of the approach rests on its bilingual design, which allows teachers to score both languages using a single rubric. The bilingual rubric includes qualitative and quantitative components. The qualitative components allow teachers to classify students' approximations at various levels, from discourse and paragraphs to words. The rubrics are designed to identify recurrent patterns of use and provide feedback to teachers who need to identify the most problematic areas for students. The quantitative components aim to score content, punctuation and spelling, which are not equally weighted, as the ability to deliver content is considered more important than the ability to spell correctly. Content carries a maximum of 7 points: punctuation 3 and spelling 4 (Escamilla *et al.*, 2014, 2018). Writing samples are collected once a year so that development can be monitored longitudinally.

The potential of using rubrics that can simultaneously score two or three languages was also explored in the Basque Country. Cenoz *et al.* (2013) discuss a very interesting study on writing skills that involved comparing students' assessment scores in English, Basque and Spanish, using monolingual, bilingual and trilingual indexes. Participants ($n = 57$) were secondary school students in Model D schools, i.e. schools with Basque as the language of instruction and Spanish and English as regular school subjects. Using questionnaires, participants provided information on their language background, after which they were given a picture description task and were asked to write three compositions on different days, one in each language (Basque, English and Spanish). Based on a scoring rubric for English as a second language (ESL) compositions, developed by Jacobs *et al.* (1981), the study initially scored writing in each individual language on five different dimensions: content, organisation, vocabulary, language use and mechanics. Two further indexes were used for comparison purposes: a bilingual index which added the scores of Basque and Spanish and a trilingual index which added the scores of Basque, Spanish and English. Overall, no significant differences in performance were found when texts were assessed using the bilingual or multilingual score indexes, while significant differences were found between groups of speakers with different L1s (Spanish and Basque) when scores were assigned to individual languages. These findings therefore suggest that monolingual scoring can provide very different results when compared to bilingual or multilingual scoring and that adopting greater flexibility in scoring can bring positive changes to the testing process.

The study provides an important contribution to the field on two key aspects of assessment: the potential that multilingual scoring rubrics can offer and the negative implications of using monolingual scoring rubrics with multilingual populations. Multilingual scoring offers an interesting alternative to monolingual scoring and is a good initial response to the frequent suggestion that multilinguals should be allowed to use all the resources available to them during the testing process. Multilingual rubrics, however, cannot be easily used in all contexts and leave open the thorny question of how they can be systematically introduced into multilingual classrooms with students who speak several different languages. A trilingual education programme could easily devise multilingual rubrics including all teaching languages, but this would not solve the problem of submitting immigrant students with different L1s to unfair assessment practices, as not all languages can be represented within the same set of rubrics.

If the use of monolingual rubrics raises concerns about unfairness and inequality in assessment, the use of multilingual rubrics that include only the languages of instruction raises similar concerns and for the same reasons. Despite the limitations, however, multilingual scoring offers a level of flexibility that can be very useful in many multilingual educational contexts. Although a multilingual scoring rubric is likely to include only the official languages of instruction, some immigrant students who do not know how to express themselves in a given language may still find it very helpful to be given the opportunity to do so using words and expressions in one of the other languages of instruction used in the school. In large-scale testing, multilingual scoring would be more difficult to implement but not impossible. For instance, students could be given the opportunity to use the language of testing and perhaps one other language, i.e. their most dominant language, and answers could then be scored by bilingual raters with knowledge of the two languages. This would require more extensive organisation for testing agencies, but bilingual raters should not be too difficult to locate and train for scoring purposes.

4.2.2 Test instructions and answers in multiple languages

Connected to the discussion of multilingual scoring is the problem that students with poor knowledge of the language of testing may not be able to understand the test instructions and, as a result, may not be able to answer one or more of the questions asked. Lack of comprehension is a very common problem in testing. One of the solutions considered has been to give students test instructions in two languages and/or give them the possibility of answering test items in one of their two languages or both (Gandara & Randall, 2019; Levin & Shohamy, 2008; López et al., 2017, 2019). Most of the research studies available are focused on bilinguals, so the effectiveness and feasibility of these practices when three or more languages are involved remain unknown.

An example of these practices comes from the work that Gandara and Randall (2019) conducted with bilingual children in the Republic of Congo. The authors worked with a total of 80 children from third to sixth grade attending four different schools located in the city of Mbandaka, in the Province of Equateur. Living conditions in the area are quite harsh and the local population faces many challenges associated with both poverty and the hot climate. In this context, education is a challenge by itself and language choice is only one of the challenges students and teachers are likely to face in school.

The children who attend local schools speak Lingala and French, the official language of instruction. Aiming to identify the best linguistic option for these children, Gandara and Randall chose to focus on the Early Grade Mathematics Assessment (EGMA) tests. Half of the children were assigned to a translingual EGMA group; the other half to a traditional EGMA group. In the traditional EGMA, participants were asked to choose either French or Lingala for maths assessment, while children assigned to the translingual group received instruction in French and/or Lingala (translingual EGMA) and were asked to respond in either of their two languages. The results were quite encouraging, as the translingual version was found to be superior to the traditional one and, above all, to be very effective in helping children improve their performance. The authors consequently argued that test instructions in two languages and/or giving students the possibility of answering test items in more than one language is a useful approach to assessment. For these children, it was clearly important to achieve a better understanding of the test items, since French was the language of instruction, but the children were used to speaking a different language within their community.

Equally inspiring results, but for different reasons, were obtained by López et al. (2019), who also discussed the positive outcomes associated with allowing English and Spanish bilingual students to answer maths test items using both their languages. Within a translanguaging framework, the authors took the position that students should be able to access their entire linguistic repertoire during the completion of a test. This led them to focus on the role of language support and the modality of input and output in testing. The authors created a test which, in addition to the use of Spanish and English, introduced the use of the four language skills for communication. Integrated language support was made available for receptive skills (seeing or listening to a test item), productive skills (providing written or oral answers) and vocabulary (access to synonyms in English, Spanish or both languages). At the end of the test, the authors also held follow-up interviews with the students, who confirmed the importance of being able to use multiple language resources and receive different types of language support during the completion of the test. Overall, the study further confirms the usefulness of a bilingual approach to maths assessment. The authors also stress the importance of providing instruction in more than one modality (oral and written) and argue in favour of the use of technology for assessment purposes because of the general flexibility it can offer.

Providing instructions and/or accepting answers in more than one language is a useful approach, but when the same approach is extended to heterogeneous classroom contexts, it can be readily understood how difficult it would be to implement it in most contexts. Schools would need a substantial budget for translations into multiple languages and to pay teachers with the necessary language competence to grade students' answers, so this solution is likely too expensive to be seriously considered, though it may be more feasible for larger testing services with more funding available. Furthermore, as López et al. (2019) suggest, the use of technology could offer considerable flexibility to students, who would be able to read and listen to test items and give oral or written answers in the languages of their choice. Organising computer-based testing for large numbers of learners poses great challenges, but in most educational contexts the technology is already available and is likely to become even more commonplace and accessible in the future, so this is not a solution to be discarded without further research on its potential use in testing.

4.2.3 Testing accommodations and the use of students' L1

The field of testing accommodations has been extremely active due to the widespread interest in finding effective solutions for children and adolescents with disabilities (Pitoniak & Royer, 2001; Sireci *et al.*, 2005). Several researchers have also focused on the potential use of accommodations for healthy immigrants and minority language speakers (Willner & Mokhtari, 2017), aiming to help them improve their test scores when proficiency in the language of testing is still low (for a meta-analysis, see Kieffer *et al.*, 2009).

The fields of testing accommodations and bilingualism have been linked since Cummins' seminal work on bilingual children in education. Long before, Cummins (1980, 1984) had identified a clear link between the excessive number of bilingual children being referred to special needs services and children's low proficiency in the language of instruction. His work helped raise awareness about the problem of overreferrals, and since then improvements have been reported, but more recent research also indicates that the proportion of referred bilingual children continues to be higher than would normally be expected (Artiles *et al.*, 2005; Rhodes *et al.*, 2005; Sullivan *et al.*, 2009).

Test accommodations are broadly defined as 'adaptations that are made to the design of an assessment or its administration that do not alter the measurement of the underlying construct or the interpretations of the scores on that assessment' (International Test Commission, 2019: 328). Researchers generally agree that testing accommodations are useful in testing (Abedi *et al.*, 2005), but not all types of accommodations have been found to be equally effective and construct validity has also been questioned.

In a meta-analysis that focused on several types of accommodations such as language simplification, tests being offered in the native language, giving additional time to students and the use of dictionaries, glossaries, dual-language test booklets and dual questions, Kieffer *et al.* (2009) found that, apart from the use of bilingual glossaries and dictionaries, testing accommodations were not particularly effective. Young *et al.* (2008) claimed that bilingual glossaries and word lists are effective types of accommodation, and Duncan *et al.* (2005) provided evidence that dual-language booklets are also useful. Abedi *et al.* (2005) also focused on accommodations and found that accommodations are not equally effective across school grades, which may explain the inconsistency of some of the results. If we are to shed more light on the effectiveness of certain types of accommodations, it would therefore be appropriate to consider the various types of accommodations in relation to school grades and the age of the students. Other scholars have also raised further questions about test accommodations that focus on the notion of construct validity, arguing that accommodations can significantly alter the underlying construct of a test (De Backer *et al.*, 2017; Johnson & Monroe, 2004; Schissel, 2014).

Among the various types of testing accommodations that are of most relevance to immigrants and minority language speakers are language accommodations, which assume that language support will improve students' understanding of the language of testing (Abedi *et al.*, 2005; López *et al.*, 2017). Language accommodations are based on the fundamental assumption that it is possible for us to identify what makes a test difficult and that we can address the problem by creating an easier version of the same test without violating construct validity and therefore the integrity of the test. Differential item functioning (DIF) is often employed to identify the complexity of a test (Allalouf *et al.*, 1999; Haag *et al.*, 2013; Heppt *et al.*, 2014; Martiniello, 2008; Young *et al.*, 2008).

Adaptations refer to the 'changes that are made to the design of an assessment in terms of content, format or test administration to increase access to the material on the assessment for cultural or linguistic groups that may differ from the mainstream population' (International Test Commission, 2019: 328–329). Adaptations are therefore regarded as central to ensuring that test materials and/or instructions are made more accessible to linguistically and culturally diverse student populations. Adaptations can range from simplifying or translating test content and test items to providing subject-specific glossaries and word lists. Language simplification is a type of accommodation that involves the adaptation of test content or test instructions, in which simplification can be achieved by using high frequency vocabulary and simple grammar (Johnson & Monroe, 2004) and/or the use of references that can be easily understood by culturally diverse groups (International Test Commission, 2019). Some forms of accommodation are external to the test and function as aids to the comprehension process, for instance dictionaries or bilingual glossaries, while other forms relate to simplifying the test and involve direct manipulation of content.

Language accommodations reflect what teachers instinctively do in the classroom when they try to help students understand academic content. While most teachers have used teacher talk in their work and adopted strategies such as giving preference to high frequency words, using short, simple sentences or opting for simple grammar (Bristol, 2015; Kim & Elder, 2005; Rix, 2009; Takahashi-Breines, 2002), it is perhaps too optimistic to assume that this type of teacher behaviour occurs regularly in the classroom. De Backer *et al.* (2017) provided interesting evidence in this regard. The authors set out to identify the most common practices used by primary and secondary schoolteachers in Flanders, Belgium. In the context of the MARS project, they interviewed 30 schoolteachers, many of whom confirmed their use of language-based simplification strategies in their work, such as splitting double questions or asking short and simple questions. The authors, however, also found that teachers' attitudes towards the use of accommodations varied substantially from teacher to teacher, as did the actual use of accommodations in class.

The use of simplification can be very important in disciplines that use complex vocabulary to refer to complex notions. Learning maths in different languages, for instance, can be a very challenging task because of the specialised lexicon that is used, which also increases in difficulty as the student progresses through different levels of education (Abedi & Gándara, 2006; Gandara & Randall, 2019). Minority language speakers may find learning subject-specific vocabulary particularly demanding and may not understand an entire test question due to lack of adequate language competence. Martiniello (2008) provides some good examples of these difficulties in a study that examined the Massachusetts Comprehensive Assessment System (MCAS) fourth-grade maths test, which is taken by native and non-native speakers of English. The study was carried out in the United States, where people who speak a minority language are mainly native speakers of Spanish. Martiniello claimed that students with an equal level of maths proficiency could not do equally well in the test due to the language difficulties embedded in the test. The author analysed the complexity of the test items and also used some think-aloud protocols with students. Linguistic complexity was measured by focusing on structural complexity, such as the association between words, verbs, phrases, clauses and so forth, and lexical complexity, that is, those words that might have been difficult for a non-native speaker to understand. Among the examples mentioned, he discusses the case of a question that reads as follows:

> To win a game, Tamika must spin an even number on a spinner identical to the one shown below [picture of a round spinner with 10 equal slices and random numbers from 1 to 10 is represented]. Are Tamika's chances of spinning an even number certain, likely, unlikely, or impossible? (Martiniello, 2008: 342)

The author comments on the complexity of the item, which he claims could be very confusing for non-native speakers, stating that

> the first sentence starts with an introductory adverbial clause that includes a nonpersonal form of a verb (to win). The main clause starts with an uncommon proper noun (Tamika) that functions as subject. The verbal phrase displays a complex verb that includes the modal verb must,

a noun phrase as a direct object (an even number), and a highly complex prepositional phrase with an embedded adjectival phrase that includes the past participle shown. (Martiniello, 2008: 343)

The think-aloud interviews also provided some additional input about language difficulties. Martiniello (2008) reports that some Spanish L1 children did not understand what a spinner was and, in fact, did not understand the question at all, because they understood the information 'identical to the one shown below' to mean that the question had something to do with the numeral 1 shown in the picture of the spinner. Comprehension was clearly an issue for the students, and misunderstandings of this kind illustrate how low proficiency in the language of testing can impact performance, a view that is shared by many other scholars in the field (Abedi, 2006; Abedi & Gándara, 2006; Abedi et al., 2001; Gandara & Randall, 2019). Part of the problem is that test writers are not trained to write for non-native speakers and may require awareness training to learn about the potential areas of difficulty these students may encounter. They may also need some practice in the use of language simplification strategies in order not to alter the meaning of a test and to avoid compromising test validity (Abedi, 2006).

Abedi and Lord (2001) conducted another very interesting study on the role of language in maths assessment and how language can affect students' understanding of word problems. The authors discussed data collected during different field studies, and their participants ($n = 1174$, eighth-grade students in the United States) included non-native speakers of English as well as native speakers of English of different socioeconomic backgrounds. Participants were given original and simplified test items from the National Assessment of Educational Progress mathematics assessment test, and some students were also interviewed. Among the simplifications introduced were vocabulary adaptations that were selected based on frequency of use and level of familiarity, and abstract terms were turned into concrete terms. Other forms of simplification concerned grammar and structure and included the transformation of passive into active verbs, the separation of conditional clauses, the reformulation of relative clauses and the simplification of complex questions. Descriptions were also shortened. When the authors compared the students' scores on the original and the simplified test items, they found that the students scored better on the simplified items. Interestingly, the simplified items were also easier for non-native speakers of English to use as well as for those native speakers who were low performers and of low socioeconomic status. Writing tests using simple language and simple sentence structure, in other words, is a good practice that can be useful to all students taking a test, not only the non-native speakers with objective language difficulties.

Another accommodation strategy widely used in testing is translation. A great deal of research on the effectiveness of translation as an accommodation strategy has been carried out in areas with large and homogeneous groups of minority language speakers. Some areas of the United States, for instance, are typical locations for research on this type of accommodation and for examples of its use in standardised testing. In New York, translations are already available for major standardised tests, for instance the Regents Examinations in maths, science and social studies, with translations available in several languages such as Spanish, Korean, Chinese, Haitian Creole and Russian (Menken, 2008). Large standardised tests such as the PISA test are also provided in translation. With regard to the effectiveness of translation as an accommodation strategy, the evidence is mixed. Some studies have shown evidence in its support (Robinson, 2010), others have claimed there is insufficient evidence to be able to reach a positive conclusion (Turkan & Oliveri, 2014) and yet others have provided evidence that translation is not linked to improved performance (Ong, 2013).

A central question about the use of translation in testing relates to whether students should be exposed to academic content in the translated language or in the original language of instruction. While translations can be very useful for general comprehension, Turkan and Oliveri (2014) maintain it would be important to provide access to both the original and the translated instructions or content, as some students may not be familiar with discipline-specific vocabulary in their L1 or may not even be literate in their L1, in which case recordings may be used. Translations can also be used to create bilingual glossaries and word lists (Young *et al.*, 2008) and dual-language test booklets (Duncan *et al.*, 2005), both of which have been found to be effective. Translations are also usually provided in writing, but it is not uncommon for teachers to provide oral translations as well if needed (Stansfield, 2011).

Testing accommodations are also frequently discussed in relation to the use of technology for test administration, as technology offers test takers the flexibility to consult different resources in languages that are more familiar to them, using tools such as dictionaries or grammars while taking the test. López *et al.* (2019), for instance, showed a good example of how learners can be provided with language support and use different modalities of communication (reading, speaking, listening and writing) while taking a test.

On the whole, the use of translations in testing can be said to be helpful for a range of purposes, but as an accommodation strategy translations are very difficult to use and implement without financial support, as the higher the number of languages that need to be translated, the more expensive the use of translation becomes. Translations also require substantial work to ensure item equivalence across languages. Large-scale international testing agencies regularly use translation for assessment purposes (Hambleton, 2001; Hambleton *et al.*, 2004) and provide strict and well-designed guidelines to aid the translation process (OECD, 2018). Several studies have nonetheless raised considerable concerns about the inconsistency of translations and have questioned item equivalence and the quality of translation processes (Arffman, 2013; Ercikan, 1998; Maxwell, 1996; Solano-Flores *et al.*, 2016; Zhao *et al.*, 2018), as well as the limited training translators receive (Upsing & Rittberger, 2018).

Given the disadvantages associated with testing in students' non-dominant languages, some studies have focused on the effect of using monolingual tests, this time not in the official languages of instruction but in the students' mother tongues. Gorter and Cenoz (2017), for instance, report on a study conducted in the Basque Country which provides good insights into the importance of testing minority language speakers using their native language. ISEI-IVEI (2012) analysed different standardised test results, including the PISA test results, focusing on whether any differences arose when students were tested in the L1 or the L2. The students examined were attending Basque-medium schools, so they were all learning subjects through Basque, with the exceptions of English and Spanish, which were taught as regular subjects. A pattern of higher results was shown in maths, reading and science when students were tested in their L1, confirming what many scholars have claimed over the years: testing students in a language that is not their L1 will put them at a disadvantage. Another study that examined the same difference, this time in the Canadian context, was carried out by Fox and Cheng (2007), who focused on the Ontario Secondary School Literacy Test (OSSLT) and students' perceptions of the test construct. The study, which involved 33 focus groups of 22 native speakers and 136 non-native English speakers, all attending Ontario secondary schools, found large differences between L1 and L2 accounts of the same test construct, which led the authors to argue that native and non-native speakers interpret the test construct differently, with substantial implications for testing.

Acknowledging that testing a student in the mother tongue is better and more effective than testing him/her in an L2 can be useful to raise awareness of the importance of not neglecting the student's language profile and of not comparing students who have different language profiles. It is, however, unrealistic to think that tests can always be provided in students' native languages on every occasion. As already discussed earlier in this chapter, translations involve considerable costs and substantial management difficulties that only large testing agencies can afford. Moreover, translations do not exonerate agencies from considering that students with different language profiles should not be compared to one other. A step towards a solution would be to introduce systematic comparisons between students with comparable language profiles.

Overall, discussions of the use of testing accommodations for L2 speakers remain under scrutiny as researchers do not seem to be in full agreement about their usefulness in education. The field of testing accommodations for multilinguals is instead a blank slate and some types of accommodations may not be easy to implement when more than two or three languages are involved.

4.3 Focusing on the Test Takers: Grouping by Language Background and Community Languages

The focus of this section is on two factors known to influence test scores: individual language profiles and languages spoken in the community. The section explores how the field of multilingual testing and assessment has dealt with these two factors so far and how our understanding of their effect on language development can be used to improve existing assessment practices.

The use of monolingual tests in education is often described as unfair to immigrant students and to people who speak a minority language, because students with very different language profiles are likely to perform differently on the same test. Finding a way to manage the heterogeneity of the student population is thus an important issue for testing and assessment, because those who speak the language of testing as their mother tongue will undoubtedly have an advantage in completing a test in their L1, and a test that gives an advantage to one group and not another is a biased test. For this reason, it is worth examining the attempts that have been made to avoid directly comparing students who speak the language of testing as their mother tongue and as an L2. A second factor that is also known to affect L2 development is language exposure within the community context. This factor is particularly important in areas where several languages are spoken on a regular basis but opportunities to communicate within the living community differ.

Students belonging to different language groups can show different learning patterns that can only be identified by comparing their performance by language background. The classic grouping used in most standardised tests is based on the difference between first- and second-generation immigrants and native speakers. Without diminishing the importance of distinguishing between first- and second-generation immigrants and native speakers, it is essential to recognise that this criterion is not precise enough for multilingual contexts, where students not only use different languages in their daily lives but are also exposed to different languages in the family environment, at school and within the community context. From an assessment perspective, the question is whether different amounts of language exposure can be linked to differences in academic performance.

An interesting study that grouped students ($n = 427$) according to language background was conducted in Wales, an officially bilingual region of the UK where both English and Welsh are spoken within the community. Gathercole *et al.* (2013) focused on receptive vocabulary and receptive grammar knowledge in English and Welsh and classified students according to patterns of language use in the home and the school context. For the purpose of the study, the authors established the following main categories: (1) monolinguals with knowledge of English only; (2) bilinguals with only English spoken in the home; (3) bilinguals with Welsh and English spoken in the home; and (4) bilinguals with only Welsh spoken in the home. The number and type of languages spoken in the home were thus central to the study, and results showed important differences in students' performance that could be linked to their patterns of language use. The study also provided evidence for the importance of including language exposure in normed tests, as this factor allows us to understand whether children's performance falls within the normal range for their particular cohort.

Since Gathercole and colleagues are based in a bilingual region of the UK, their investigation did not go beyond bilingualism and patterns of bilingual language development, but the differences they identified can be assumed to be even greater in multilingual contexts, where patterns of language use can vary in more substantial ways across the same region. In these contexts, immigrant students are particularly at risk of not being evaluated fairly, as they are expected to perform in school using languages they may only hear from time to time outside of the school context.

De Angelis (2014) examined such a scenario, showing the connection between patterns of language exposure within the community and immigrants' performance in a standardised test. The study aimed to compare immigrants' performance in the Italian INVALSI standardised test across different parts of South Tyrol, Italy. Regional differences were examined because the three official languages of South Tyrol are not evenly distributed across the region: speakers of German constitute the most widespread L1 group (69%), followed by the Italian-speaking (26%) and Ladin-speaking (4%) groups. The study re-examined standardised test results in conjunction with local language information for multilingual first- and second-generation immigrant children attending Italian language schools in the region.

The results of the INVALSI (2010) standardised test, administered throughout the country in 2009/2010, showed a significant difference between first- and second-generation immigrants at the national level, indicating what is generally considered a normal pattern of language development. The same difference, however, did not emerge in South Tyrol, where first- and second-generation immigrants showed very similar performance in the Italian test. The result naturally raised some concerns in the region, as students born and raised in South Tyrol were expected to perform better than those of more recent immigration. The reaction of any education board to information of this kind would have been to introduce general remedial strategies for all immigrant students throughout the region, which are costly to implement and time-consuming for teachers, students and their families. Standardised tests do not, however, consider the language practices of the community. In some areas of South Tyrol, the number of Italian speakers is negligible, so students are inevitably exposed to a minimal amount of Italian input outside of the school context. The study therefore proceeded to review the original INVALSI data in combination with local language information, and the results clearly identified an association between community language practices and students' performance in the Italian INVALSI test. The findings showed that taking standardised test results at face value may not be sufficient and may ultimately lead to the introduction of remedial strategies that are not suitably targeted. Overall, the study provided evidence that separating the results of standardised tests from the multilingual sociolinguistic context in which schools are located does not provide reliable information and does not offer any benefit to the education system that is actively trying to meet the needs of students of recent immigration.

Dividing students according to language background and languages spoken within the community ensures that minority language speakers are compared with minority language speakers of similar profiles, monolinguals with monolinguals, multilinguals with multilinguals and so forth. Groups of students may vary from context to context and training a generation of teachers and educators to conceptualise assessment according to students' prior language background and living environment will help them get accustomed to the idea of interpreting test results on the basis of students' language profiles. This will also help them understand that performance can be examined according to group membership and that the division into groups ensures that no one is disadvantaged and, above all, that the needs of a particular group can come to light with less ambiguity.

The testing industry does not yet recognise the importance of languages spoken within a community and of test takers' individual language profiles, even though both factors are well known to influence the speed and rate of language acquisition (for a review, see De Angelis, 2007). Going beyond the simple distinction between first- and second-generation immigrants by including more information about students' backgrounds and their living environment is not technically difficult and would certainly be a step forward towards fairer and more accurate forms of assessment.

No test is unfair in itself; what is unfair is the way tests are used in education. Comparisons between students with different language profiles inevitably lead to inequalities that are of no use to anyone, while improving tests to allow more accurate comparisons would give schools, students and their families the opportunity to better interpret the meaning of test scores. Rethinking the way results are interpreted is therefore critical. Students with a similar profile should be compared to one another rather than against a hypothetical norm, and the overall results of a class or school should include a balanced proportion of students from similar language backgrounds.

In areas with large numbers of immigrants, it is not uncommon to hear that students' poor performance on standardised tests is due to the presence of large numbers of immigrant students attending the same school. This may or may not be true, but what is certain is that in standardised tests it would make more sense if the overall score of a class or school included a consistent percentage of scores from immigrant students, native speakers and functional bilinguals or multilinguals. In other words, including a specific percentage of students according to linguistic membership would help reduce inequalities and reports of injustice. In multilingual contexts, the extra layer of community languages should also be added, so that the reasons for results deviating from the norm can be easily identified.

5 Developing Tests for Multilingual Populations

The need to develop tests that are suitable for students with different language profiles is not new, but much of the work carried out so far has only involved bilingual populations, often in homogeneous contexts. As little research with multilinguals is currently available, there is a substantial gap in the literature and therefore limited guidance on how to design tests that show sufficient sensitivity to different languages and cultures and that can also be evaluated and interpreted fairly.

Several authors have highlighted the need to identify test writing strategies that are inclusive and therefore suitable for students of different profiles (Fairbairn & Fox, 2009; Green, 1997; Hambleton et al., 2004; Nortvedt et al., 2020; Ortiz et al., 2012; Rhodes et al., 2005), and some detailed guidelines on large-scale assessment have already been published (International Test Commission, 2019). While guidelines are an important step forward as they recognise the need to make tests more accessible, they only represent a partial solution to the problem as they do not take multilingual individuals, their language background and their living environment into consideration when tests are scored and interpreted.

It should not be forgotten that a test does not end with the student's score but with its interpretation. A test score provides information about the student's progress and performance, but an incorrectly interpreted test score does not provide information that can be regarded as useful or reliable. One way to improve current practices would be to pay more attention to the difference between writing tests for multilingual populations and testing multilingual individuals. Both tests and test takers are an integral part of the assessment process and considerations relating to both should form the basis of every decision made. In practice, this means that tests must not only be designed with sufficient sensitivity towards linguistically and culturally diverse students but must also be scored and interpreted using all relevant information about the test takers. Without this last step, unfairness and inequality are likely to occur.

Some have argued that the considerable economic and political interests behind the national and international testing industry have been slowing down progress towards more equitable forms of assessment (Dendrinos, 2019; Shohamy, 2011). Making tests linguistically simpler or culturally neutral is a solution that is certainly favourable to the testing industry which, thanks to these adaptations, can continue to provide monolingual tests without compromising its influence and economic benefits. This measure is, however, insufficient, as the adaptation of a test focuses only on the test, without taking into consideration test takers' profiles and their usual place of residence.

The integrated approach to testing and assessment is conceived as responding to this problem, which is addressed by placing both the test and the test taker at the heart of its conceptualisation. The approach is referred to as *integrated* because it combines information about the test and the test takers, as both types of information are regarded as essential to the assessment process. As previously defined, an integrated approach to testing and assessment is an approach that refers to the process of gathering information about the knowledge, skills and abilities of multilingual learners, using tools *designed* for linguistically and culturally diverse populations that may be *administered* in multiple modalities, *scored* by multilingual examiners and *interpreted* using data about the test takers that includes information about their language background and living environment. The four key components of the approach thus revolve around the multilingual individual and the way the test is designed, administered, scored and interpreted.

A distinctive feature of the approach is its flexibility, in that each stage of test design is conceived as an individual block or unit that allows the test writer to make linguistic decisions that can range from monolingualism to multilingualism, depending on the test profile, i.e. the purpose of the test, the test construct and the population to be tested. This chapter offers recommendations for each of the four phases, i.e. design, administration, scoring and interpretation, and aims to provide a general framework for test development that can be readily used by teachers, test writers and educators working with multilingual student populations, as well as for training purposes. The recommendations are non-technical in nature and have been written with the full awareness that each step of the process deserves to be further developed through empirical research with students. Until this is possible, these recommendations can be used for initial guidance and support. The test writer is also guided through the main issues that need to be considered when writing a test for multilingual students. Some examples are given, with the objective of increasing the general awareness of what each phase requires and the types of options that are available. Guidance questions are also included in each section to help decisions at each stage of the process.

5.1 Design

5.1.1 Defining the purpose of testing, the test construct and the population of interest

The first step in test development is to identify the purpose of testing, the type of construct to be measured and the target population. These decisions provide an initial test profile that will inform all the decisions that follow.

What is the purpose of testing?

Assessment broadly refers to the process of collecting information about students' performance and progress using a range of different methods or tests that can be administered for different purposes and at different times of the year. The variety of tests in the field of education is extremely wide, as is their purpose. Tests can range from large-scale international or national standardised tests designed to evaluate the quality of the education system, to school or classroom tests that can include anything from classroom presentations to end-of-year examinations, portfolios, term papers, short tests and project work. The teacher may also consider having tests carried out individually, in pairs or in groups. The purpose of testing should therefore be clearly identified early in the design process, as this will inform many of the decisions that will be taken. The tests that most teachers write for their students are likely to be classified as formative, summative or diagnostic, and a description of how these forms of assessment differ in purpose and function can be found in Chapter 1 (Section 1.3).

What is the test meant to measure?

Test writers must clearly identify what the test is meant to measure at an early stage of the design process, i.e. they must ensure the test being written has good construct validity (Cherryholmes, 1988; Strauss & Smith, 2009). Does the test measure language or content? Does the test measure factual knowledge, or does it aim to evaluate students' ability to analyse or infer information from a text? Is the test measuring higher-order thinking skills (HOTS) or lower-order thinking skills (LOTS) (Anderson & Krathwohl, 2001; Krathwohl, 2002)?

The notion of construct validity was originally proposed by Cronbach and Meehl (1955) in their seminal paper 'Construct Validity in Psychological Tests'. Construct validity refers to the process of evaluating the procedures that are used to measure a given construct. Construct validity is a complex notion that most teachers are not trained to recognise, so I shall attempt to describe its relevance using an example on climate change. Suppose a teacher wants to assess whether students understand climate change (the construct). The teacher prepares a reading comprehension test using two short descriptions of climate changes over the last 40 years. She/he then instructs the students to complete two tasks (the measurement) by asking them to (a) create a graph that illustrates the climate changes that have occurred over the past 40 years and (b) describe the cause–effect relationships, for example the association between global warming and rising sea levels. The teacher then scores the graphs and the descriptions using predefined criteria (e.g. the presence or absence of a list of changes, the cause–effect relationship between the different elements and so forth). To assess the validity of the construct, the teacher should then ask: Do the texts provide enough information to assess whether the student understands climate change over the last 40 years? Is the information provided relevant for the construct being tested? Are the climate changes explicitly stated, or is the student expected to infer them from the texts? Is there information that is more relevant for an additional question? Are the assessment criteria precise enough to measure the student's ability to understand climate change over the period in question? Early attention to construct validity can be very useful for teachers and test writers who want to ensure that the content chosen for a test is suitable for the questions being asked.

Does the target population include culturally and linguistically diverse students? Can students be grouped according to language background and/or by languages spoken in the community?

If the target population includes culturally and linguistically diverse students, the test writer must first determine whether students can be classified as a heterogeneous or a homogeneous group. In a Californian classroom, for example, the student population may be homogeneous, with Spanish and English as the two main languages spoken in the classroom, but if the test is taken by students of more than one class, the chances are that not all students will have a similar language profile and therefore that the group will be heterogeneous rather than homogeneous. The type of student population found in Ladin schools in South Tyrol, Italy, is a good example of a heterogeneous group. The number of languages spoken by students in the same classroom can vary considerably, as most students will be familiar with the three languages of instruction (Ladin, German and Italian) to different levels of proficiency, and students of immigrant origin may also speak other languages in the family context.

It is essential to stop and think about who the test takers are at a very early stage of the design process for two reasons. First, if the test is taken by a homogeneous group, for example a group of Spanish and English students, language choices based only on these two languages can be safely made. If the group is heterogeneous, language choices will be much more complex, and the test design will require more careful consideration. Second, the identification of group membership determines whether students can be divided according to language background and/or the languages spoken within the community (see also Section 2.3.3).

The division of students according to group membership is a crucial step in the design process and should not be underestimated. If the test is a standardised test, it will be necessary to collect information about the students' language background and the languages spoken in the community. In the case of immigrants, in addition to home language practices, information on the age of arrival in the host country will also be essential. If the test is for a local school or a classroom, teachers should ensure that students' profiles and their language practices within the family environment and the community are fully documented, as this information will be relevant when interpreting the test.

5.1.2 Choosing the test format

Which is the most suitable test format?

A test can take three formats: (a) monolingual, (b) multilingual-by-translation and (c) multilingual-by-design.

Monolingual tests are tests with instructions and content provided orally or in writing in one language. Students must answer all the questions in the language of testing and only answers provided in one language are accepted. The use of monolingual tests with multilinguals remains highly controversial (see Section 4.1).

Multilingual-by-translation tests are monolingual tests fully translated into multiple languages. This is the case, for instance, with standardised tests such as PISA, which are administered in local languages throughout the world (OECD, 2010, 2012) and the Regents Examinations in maths, science and social studies, which are administered in the State of New York, USA, and are offered in a translated format for certain languages, such as Spanish, Korean, Chinese, Haitian Creole and Russian (Menken, 2008).

The feasibility of using a multilingual-by-translation format is dictated by the financial resources available to pay for translations and the quality control required to ensure construct validity is not compromised during the translation process. Funds are also required to pay the examiners, who must have the necessary language competence to grade the test. With this type of format, students have the opportunity to be tested in the language in which they feel most comfortable, and this can be useful when they have little knowledge of the language of testing and do not have the necessary language skills to understand the test questions and answer them as required. When using this format, it would be important to allow access to the test in both the source language and the translated language. Students may have learned a subject in the source language and, if the test is taken in their first language (L1), even though it may be a dominant language for them, they may not know the discipline-specific vocabulary they need in order to understand and answer the questions appropriately (Turkan & Oliveri, 2014). If students are given simultaneous access to two languages, it is also essential that the test layout does not change. If, for instance, a question in the original source language is on one page, students would be confused to find the same question in a different language presented on different pages. If the bilingual version is used, it would also be useful to consider giving students extra time so that they can easily consult the questions and content in the two languages without having to feel rushed during the test.

Multilingual-by-design tests are designed and written in more than one language. For example, instructions can be in one language and content in another, and answers can be accepted in more than one language. The possible combinations are many, and the extent and type of language mixing and the number of languages involved are decided during the design phase of the test, depending on general needs and the purpose of testing. This format is often chosen in homogeneous bilingual contexts where teachers and students are familiar with the same languages. The format can also be easily used in multilingual teaching contexts by using the official languages of instruction, while the same format is more difficult to apply whenever more than two or three languages must be included in the same test.

As language mixing is not frequently encountered in testing, test writers must ensure that students are familiar with this particular test format, which should reflect the pedagogical practices to which students have been exposed during the school year. In a trilingual school, for instance, if reading comprehension has been taught using translanguaging pedagogical strategies, students would feel very comfortable completing a test that presents instructions in language A and content in language B and requires answers in language C. If the same format is used in a monolingual teaching context without a prior familiarisation phase, however, students may feel puzzled and confused, and lack of familiarity will inevitably affect their performance.

5.1.3 Making language choices

In which language(s) are instructions and content going to be provided? In which language(s) will answers be accepted?

Test writers must make considerable language choices at an early stage, depending on the test format they have chosen. In the case of monolingual tests, the only decision to be made concerns the language of testing, i.e. the language that will be used for instructions and content and that students will be allowed to use for their answers.

Multilingual-by-translation tests are essentially monolingual tests translated into one or more languages, so the test writer must choose the main language of testing (the source language) as well as the language(s) into which the test will be translated, which could be one or several. While the use of translations seems to offer a simple solution to a complex problem, in reality this is a difficult and often expensive solution which is not viable in most educational contexts. In addition to being strongly criticised for keeping the use of monolingual tests in place with students from different language backgrounds, this solution presents considerable financial challenges for the industry as translations and quality control are expensive. Moreover, item equivalence, construct validity and the quality of translation processes have been widely questioned (Arffman, 2013; Ercikan, 1998; Gierl, 2000; Maxwell, 1996; Solano-Flores *et al.*, 2016; Zhao *et al.*, 2018), as has the limited amount of training translators receive (Upsing & Rittberger, 2018). Nonetheless, translations remain widely used in testing (Hambleton, 2001; Hambleton *et al.*, 2004; OECD, 2018) whenever financial resources permit.

The multilingual-by-design format is perhaps the most complex to design, as there is no standard way of mixing languages for assessment purposes; however, it is also the most promising option of the three because of the flexibility it offers, allowing the test writer to choose what to present and in which language.

The use of multiple languages is widely assumed to facilitate both comprehension and production processes and, with this format, instructions and content can be provided in one or more languages. The test can therefore be designed very differently depending on the choices the test writer wishes to make, which depend on the purpose of testing, the construct to be measured and the student population, i.e. the core components outlined at the beginning of this chapter as part of the test profile. Whether the test writer is a teacher or a large testing agency, this is the stage during which decisions have to be made about the extent of language mixing to be introduced in the test, the sections involved and why multiple languages are needed.

The test writer must also determine the scoring criteria and whether answers in more than one language can be accepted. In case of answers in multiple languages, an essential step is to decide to what extent other languages can be used, as mixing can range from the use of an occasional word to an entire sentence or paragraph in one or more languages. If a certain amount of mixing is regarded as acceptable, the test writer should also determine whether words or sentences can be accepted in any language or only in certain languages and if an answer can be given using more than two languages. The more languages that are used, the more likely it is that multiple examiners with the relevant language skills will have to be used for scoring.

Multilingual-by-design tests seem to be the best option for multilingual student populations and the most logical choice for multilingual teaching contexts where pedagogical practices already use several languages in the classroom. Despite the apparent straightforwardness, writing, administering and scoring a test of this kind can be a very challenging task due to the number of languages involved and the fact that writing such a test can take a lot of time that teachers very often do not have. Training teachers to write and use multilingual-by-design tests may, however, prove a good strategy for the future, as it will get new teachers into the habit of conceiving tests multilingually and accustomed to translanguaging testing practices.

5.1.4 Choosing the test input and output modalities

What test input modalities will be used for the test content and test instructions? What output modality will students be asked to use when answering the test questions?

The term *test input* is broadly used here to refer to all the test materials that are presented to students, i.e. both the instructions and the content of a test, while the term *test output* refers to all the answers given by the test takers.

The test input can be delivered to students in a number of different modalities. Input may be written or oral and may ask students to engage in listening and reading activities that can be complemented by the use of videos, audio, visual images of various kinds (pictures, graphs or drawings) and subtitles with text in the same language as the audio or in a different language. The choices made in this phase can make a considerable difference in producing a test that is suitable or unsuitable for culturally and linguistically diverse student populations.

A range of measures can be used to simplify a test and make it easier to understand for those who have weaker knowledge of the language of testing. For example, a multilingual student who is asked to read content that is too difficult to understand may greatly benefit from using image-based stimuli or watching videos with subtitles. In disciplines such as mathematics, the use of mathematical symbols, diagrams and graphs can be used instead of wordy explanations. Silent videos can also be very useful to help students understand content without relying on language knowledge.

Instructions and content may be provided in writing in several languages, and the same instructions or content may also be pre-recorded in one or more languages. The use of technology can greatly facilitate this type of delivery. An excellent example of how different modalities of input can be used with the help of technology can be seen in a mathematical test designed by López *et al.* (2019) that included dual-language support, allowing students to see or listen to the test items and to write or speak their answers.

With the exception of solutions that use more than one language, such as subtitles written in a different language from the one used for audio input, all the strategies mentioned can be used to facilitate comprehension and can make the test input more accessible. Test input modalities are closely linked to the range of accommodation strategies used to simplify a test which are widely recommended for the assessment of linguistically and culturally diverse student populations (International Test Commission, 2019; Rhodes et al., 2005).

As for the test output, the test writer needs to specify which modality the student will be asked to use to answer the test questions (spoken or written) and the most suitable answer format for the test items, such as long/short, open/closed, multiple-choice or binary-choice answers (yes/no, true/false). Above all, the test writer will need to decide whether answers can be accepted in one or more languages, perhaps using different modalities. For instance, a student may be asked to answer a test question in a non-dominant language but may also be given the possibility of providing the same answer orally in the dominant language (see López et al., 2019) or be allowed to answer orally or in writing, using two languages.

5.1.5 Writing test instructions and test items

Are test instructions and test items written using a simple vocabulary and sentence structure? Are the cultural references sufficiently neutral? Does the test contain regional language differences?

Depending on the options previously selected, at this stage the test writer starts writing the test instructions, the test items and the scoring criteria. Since scoring is an important component of multilingual-by-design tests, a discussion on scorings rubrics is provided in a later section.

Writing a test suitable for linguistically and culturally diverse student populations entails doing so with the full awareness that some students may not understand the cultural references used or may find the language load too high for their level of competence. As already discussed in several other sections of this volume, holistic approaches to testing and assessment consider the use of monolingual tests inappropriate for second language speakers. These students often lack the necessary language skills to perform well in a test, and low test results may have considerable negative implications for them, particularly in the case of high-stakes testing. This is a point of view that I fully share, and in an ideal world I would like to see more multilingual options offered in education. Despite the limitations associated with monolingual tests, however, sometimes other options are simply not possible or not available, and the reality is that multiple language speakers may be asked to take a monolingual test, even though it may not be the best option for them. It is therefore essential that all tests, regardless of format, are designed with linguistically and culturally diverse student populations in mind, which is a relatively easy goal to achieve.

The language testing industry widely supports the use of cultural and linguistic simplification in testing as the practice does not pose a threat to the continued use of monolingual tests for them, leaving many of their financial interests unaltered (Dendrinos, 2019). From an integrated approach perspective, I also share the view that cultural and linguistic simplification can be very useful in making a test more suitable for multilingual populations, regardless of whether the test is monolingual, multilingual-by-translation or multilingual-by-design; however, I would also argue that cultural and linguistic simplification is not in itself sufficient to provide a fair testing process for all test takers. This point will be discussed in more detail later in this chapter in relation to test scores and test interpretation.

A test can be easily written by carefully monitoring its linguistic and cultural load, and the simplifications introduced must be reflected in all languages, as required by the test format. For example, instructions and content, regardless of the number of languages included in the test, may be written in short sentences, using a simple sentence structure and grammar. A test may give preference to the use of active rather than passive verbs or the use of high-frequency vocabulary with no regional language variations, rather than low-frequency vocabulary and regional expressions. A test written in English should not include words in American or British English that would not be understood in Australia or South Africa, and cultural references would also need to be neutral throughout the test and should not be offensive to anyone. All things considered, monitoring the linguistic and cultural load of a test is relatively easy to do and is therefore considered a simple and effective solution by the testing industry. Of course, there is nothing wrong with this solution, except that it is insufficient to ensure that the testing process is fair and equitable for all test takers.

5.1.6 Test answers, scoring rubrics and language

Which languages can be used to answer the test questions? Do scoring rubrics penalise the student for using multiple languages?

The next decisions are related to test answers, scoring rubrics and language. Rubrics are scoring guides that set out the criteria for grading students' tests. They include information on both the depth and quality of content that students are expected to show in their answers and are very useful tools for achieving consistency in grading. An important piece of information that must be included in scoring rubrics relates to (a) the language(s) students are expected to use to answer the test questions; and (b) the amount of flexibility allowed when the answers contain words or sentences in language(s) other than the language(s) of testing.

In the case of *monolingual* and *multilingual-by-translations* tests, students are expected to answer using the language of testing, and answers will normally be marked as incorrect whenever they include words or phrases in languages other than the language of testing. *Multilingual-by-design* tests offer the most flexible option, as a student may be asked to answer a test question in more than one language or may choose to answer in one of several languages, depending on the test design. Occasionally, students may also use words or phrases in a language that is not explicitly indicated as one of the languages allowed in the test, which may cause some hesitation in deciding whether the answer should be accepted, partially accepted or rejected. Test writers must anticipate these situations and provide clear and unequivocal guidelines for scoring.

A crucial question is whether the examiner should understand all the languages that a student might use when answering a question. Let us imagine a situation where a teacher understands Spanish but not Punjabi. It would not be fair to exercise a certain tolerance for the presence of Spanish words used to fill knowledge gaps in the language of testing but the same level of tolerance not be extended to the use of Punjabi, particularly if the decision to accept or not accept an answer depends on the teacher's rather than the student's language skills. Flexibility can be a useful principle, but it must be applied consistently so that no significant bias is introduced during the scoring process. Multilingual examiners are, of course, ideal where possible, but the more flexibility that is introduced, the more likely it is that more than one examiner or rater will need to be involved in the scoring process.

On the whole, scoring rubrics play an essential role in defining which languages students are allowed to use and the extent to which they are allowed to use them when answering a test question. The integrated approach to testing and assessment considers multilingual scoring rubrics to be an essential component of a fair testing process, as they allow a level of flexibility that can be highly valuable to those with poor language skills.

5.1.7 Translations

Does the test need to be translated into one or more languages?
Is it necessary to provide translations for instructions and content or just some of the instructions and/or of the content?

Translations can be a very controversial topic as they are perceived as a way of ensuring that monolingual tests remain in place while the needs of multilingual populations remain unmet (Dendrinos, 2019; Shohamy, 2011). A test, however, does not necessarily need to be translated in its entirety. Partial translations are also possible and even useful in some circumstances. The testing industry uses translations on a regular basis and has issued strict and well-designed guidelines to aid the translation process (International Test Commission, 2018; OECD, 2018). Several authors have nonetheless argued that translations in testing can be inconsistent and not fully reliable (Arffman, 2013; Ercikan, 1998; Maxwell, 1996; Solano-Flores et al., 2016; Zhao et al., 2018). As discussed at the beginning of this chapter, vast financial and political interests surround monolingual testing and international testing agencies, and, since such powerful forces are not going to disappear overnight, there is a need to look at translation practices more closely and evaluate whether they can be used more sensibly.

Two major large-scale multilingual-by-translation international tests are organised by the Organisation for Economic Cooperation and Development (OECD): the Programme for International Student Assessment (PISA) and the International Assessment of Adult Competencies (PIAAC). The PISA test is used to measure 15-year-olds' reading literacy and mathematical and scientific knowledge, while the PIAAC test analyses adult skills in over 40 countries with reference to literacy, numeracy and problem-solving. Both tests use questionnaires to collect socioeconomic data for screening purposes (see OECD.org). Large-scale tests such as the PISA and the PIAAC are used to monitor the quality of education and the level of literacy within the target population, and test results are typically used to inform policy changes (Upsing & Rittberger, 2018) that can affect the lives of millions of people around the world. The importance of achieving fairness in testing is therefore paramount.

Translations are generally difficult to implement for two main reasons: funding and quality control. Large-scale evaluation tests such as the PISA or the PIAAC have to allocate a substantial budget to cover translation services and training, and only large testing agencies can afford this option. Even when funding is available, the translation process needs to be closely monitored for quality and consistency. Translation equivalence goes well beyond meaning verification in the translated language, and all potential problems need to be identified before the test can be formally approved. The original and translated versions must also be of a similar size and have a similar layout, which entails that they should be of similar lengths, instructions and test items should be presented in the same position on the page and students should be asked the same number of questions. The number of staff involved in the translation of both large-scale international tests and country-specific bilingual tests is considerable, and it is easy to understand why this is a solution that not everyone can afford.

The use of translations is based on the fundamental assumption that students will find it easier to complete a test in the dominant language than in a non-dominant language. Students may indeed find it easier to use the dominant language in tests, particularly at the early stages of learning, but as they progress in their education they may also find they are not sufficiently familiar with discipline-specific vocabulary in their L1, especially if they have learned the subject in a non-dominant language. Doing a translated version of a test may therefore not always be the easiest and most advantageous choice for them. While translations are mostly used in large-scale assessment, they can also be used at the level of individual schools operating in bilingual and trilingual educational contexts, but feasibility and funding are likely to remain a major obstacle. In the absence of a specific budget for translations, it is normally the school staff who must lend themselves to the translation of a test. Knowing a language and being a teacher, however, is not the same as being a professional translator, and while teachers often have the right language skills, they may lack the training and/or the time to do a satisfactory job.

5.2 Administration

Can the test be administered as planned? Is the necessary technology available for use? Are all supporting materials available?

The test administration phase depends on the choices made during the various stages of test design and on the input and output modalities selected. At this stage, it is necessary to review the test and identify what may be necessary for its administration. The use of multiple modalities increases the complexity of test administration and is likely to require the use of technology.

To begin with the input, if audio, video, image projection or the use of subtitles have been selected, it will be necessary to ensure that the required technology is available to administer the test as expected. If, for example, a test is being completed on a computer in English but the instructions can also be heard in other pre-recorded languages, it will be necessary to check that each student has access to a computer equipped with headphones so as not to disturb other students who are completing the same test. The same must be verified for the selected output modality, especially if answers need to be recorded. In a classroom context and if the test design allows it, a teacher may also plan to translate instructions verbally and interact with the class using a language other than the language of testing. *Multilingual-by-design* tests are the most elaborate tests to administer as multiple languages are integrated into the same test. For example, a test may have instructions in one language, content in another and answers in yet another, and students may need headphones to listen to different options, particularly if they are given the possibility of choosing different parts of the test in different languages.

Another fundamental aspect involves verifying what forms of support students need. In addition to technology, it is necessary to ensure that support materials are available in different languages, such as dictionaries and glossaries, if allowed. If the teacher is expected to read the test instructions or parts of the test, it must be ensured that staff have the necessary language skills to carry out the task as intended. Pupils who speak the test language as a second language may need more time to complete the test when they are consulting dictionaries or accessing the translation of a test or part of a test. Generally, during the administrative phase of the test, one should carefully consider whether the test can be administered correctly, using all the languages included in the design and with all the forms of language support originally planned.

5.3 Scoring

*Do the scoring criteria specify in which language(s)
the student can answer the test questions?*

For multilingual speakers, scoring is an essential and crucial component of the assessment process, since it is during the scoring phase that they are compared to their monolingual peers and can therefore be penalised for their language skills.

Scoring rubrics outline the criteria that guide the entire scoring process. The use of multiple languages or taking the test in the second language hardly even feature among the assessment criteria, with inevitable consequences for those who take a test in a non-dominant language. Rubrics are typically designed to be user-friendly and to make the grading task easy to follow, consistent and effective, but the same set of criteria should not be used with all students without first considering their language background and the languages spoken in the community.

There are different types of rubrics, of which the most common are analytic and holistic. Analytic rubrics are intended to describe what the student is expected to achieve in each of the test criteria. These types of rubrics are typically presented in a grid format, with the criteria listed in the left column and the performance levels listed horizontally; each criterion is then evaluated independently. By contrast, holistic rubrics describe the overall level of performance and all the criteria are included in each level. A single score is assigned to the student's performance.

Rubrics usually include the criteria or the learning objectives against which the students' performance is measured, a scale that specifies the standards expected and the performance indicators. The objective is to provide a fair assessment process for all students, but if no distinction is made between speaker types (native speakers vs immigrants and/or minority language speakers), the score will inevitably be biased, as it is highly unlikely that the criteria and the standards specified in the rubrics will be met by those for whom the language of testing is a non-dominant language.

One of the main concerns with rubrics and language relates to finding ways of integrating the use of languages other than the language of testing. Much criticism towards monolingual rubrics arises from the fact that answers given in languages other than the language of testing are not accepted, with enormous disadvantages for immigrant and minority language speakers who may not be able to express themselves as native peers (López et al., 2017). The importance of a multilingual approach to scoring has already been highlighted in the use of bilingual scoring rubrics such as those developed within the Literacy Squared model designed in the United States, which were found to be highly effective (Escamilla et al., 2014, 2018), or in the difference found between students' assessment scores, depending on whether monolingual, bilingual or trilingual indexes are used in scoring (Cenoz et al., 2013).

Most rubrics do not envisage the use of languages other than the language of testing. If the student answers in a different language, the answer is marked as incorrect, even if the student has answered the question correctly, only with the help of another language. This raises two key issues for multilingual testing and assessment. The first concerns the possibility of accepting an answer if it contains whole words, parts of a word such as a morpheme or even short sentences in a language that is not the language of testing. If the answer is in favour of mixing languages, the second question concerns the extent to which mixing can be accepted and whether language mixing is allowed in all languages or in some languages, e.g. the languages of instruction in bilingual or trilingual education or any of the languages the students speak. This choice presupposes that the examiner understands the languages being used or that more than one examiner will be involved in scoring the test.

Clearly, several choices can be made when writing scoring rubrics for multilinguals. By keeping the target population in mind, as suggested at the beginning of this chapter, scoring rubrics can start to be developed in a way that can fit the students' profiles and their expressive skills more effectively, thus reducing the possibility of introducing a bias in the scoring process.

5.4 Interpretation

Are students being compared according to language background and, where relevant, the languages spoken within the living community?

A test score provides information about the student's learning progress and his/her performance in a given subject. A score by itself, however, is meaningless, unless performance is measured against that of a hypothetical norm (norm-referenced tests) or a set of learning objectives or criteria (criterion-referenced tests). Scoring, in other words, becomes unfair and inequitable once it is interpreted, which takes us to this last phase of the assessment process.

Students who have different language profiles and live in different language contexts learn to use their languages very differently from context to context. It is well known that the quality and quantity of input determines how much and to what extent one can learn language. From a language acquisition perspective, the languages with which students are familiar and the social context in which they are spoken are regarded as crucial for learning.

In testing, repeated objections have been raised against the practice of comparing multiple language speakers with monolingual speakers because, it is argued, multilinguals will never be able to achieve native-like competence in the language of testing and will therefore be significantly disadvantaged (López et al., 2016; Shohamy, 2011; Stavans & Hoffmann, 2015). Giving students the possibility of completing a *multilingual-by-design* test can be an excellent, albeit complex and logistically complicated solution. An even easier solution would be to stop comparing students who are clearly different in terms of language background and who may live in communities where different language practices expose them to a different quantity and quality of input.

Multilinguals should be classified and compared according to their real language profiles, not hypothetical group memberships to which they are conveniently assigned but that do not adequately represent them. A test score provides its intended meaning when like is compared with like, that is, if monolinguals are compared with monolinguals, immigrants with a certain profile with immigrants with a similar profile and so forth. In other words, the interpretation of test scores should be conceptualised by departing from the idea that students should be compared with one another because they physically share the same class or school or live in the same country. An alternative approach would be to introduce the practice of comparing students on the basis of their language profiles and, where relevant, their community context.

Multilinguals cannot be easily classified into either/or categories and doing so can have significant implications for them. A good example of where a failure to classify students in accordance with language background may lead to a highly unfair testing process is the case of those who live in multilingual contexts and are functional multilinguals, like most of the students who attend Ladin schools in South Tyrol. In standardised testing, these students cannot be classified as immigrants because neither they nor their parents or grandparents have ever moved from their place of residence. They are then treated as native speakers, even though they are being tested in a language that is not their L1, and their scores are compared with those of native speakers at national level or native speakers living in neighbouring regions. While students in Ladin schools in South Tyrol generally compare well with native speakers, asking them to perform like native speakers puts them under undue pressure to perform according to native-like standards. It would be more reasonable and more logical to measure their progress by comparing them directly with other functional multilinguals attending bilingual or multilingual education programmes within the country. With regard to immigrant children, De Angelis (2014) also showed that by focusing on patterns of language use within the living community, the same standardised test results can provide completely different information. When test scores are analysed and then interpreted in combination with local language information, differences based on community languages are clearly identifiable.

As previously stated, a test does not end with a test score but with its interpretation. Several researchers have already focused on improving testing practices for multilingual students by focusing on the scoring process and on alternative classification methods such as grouping according to language background and/or languages spoken in the living community (see Chapter 4). While research with multilingual populations is still very young and further research is needed to clarify what can be changed and how effective changes can be, focusing on the scoring and interpretation process seems to offer the highest potential for bringing substantial improvements to current testing practices.

6 Assessing Multilingual Narratives

Between 2015 and 2017, I conducted a study on multilingual narratives with multilingual children (aged 6–14) attending Ladin trilingual primary and lower secondary schools in the Province of Bolzano-Bolzen, South Tyrol, Italy. The study was conducted in cooperation with the local Ladin school board.

The South Tyrolean context is particularly fascinating for research with multilingual children, as those who attend local Ladin schools either have a migratory background or are raised speaking local minority languages, having lived in these lands for generations. The study focused on children in the former category, as these children need to learn and master three different languages of instruction (Ladin, German and Italian) to complete the trilingual school cycle successfully. Most of these children also speak a home language that differs from the three languages of instruction, so they are exposed to at least four languages by the time they start school.

In a school system of this kind, the Ladin school board was interested in learning more about the immigrant children's patterns of language development and how the three languages of instruction were interacting with one another during the developmental process. More specifically, the board wished to understand whether it would be better to introduce immigrant children to all the languages of instruction from the outset or more gradually, and how long it would take for a child to learn enough language to reach the level of their native peers in terms of educational achievement. These questions were addressed by focusing on children's narrative skills.

Narratives are oral accounts of real or imaginary events that are widely used in educational and clinical settings to assess the language and cognitive development of both monolingual and bilingual children and to identify children with specific language impairments (SLI). Narratives are considered valuable tools for assessment as they reflect how the child conceptualises, plans and organises content, all of which involves the use of both linguistic and cognitive skills. Narratives are widely used with both typically developing (TD) children and children with SLI to observe the use of language in context and examine the level of lexical and grammatical development in each of the child's languages. Narratives also show whether the child has developed the ability to use the basic elements of story grammar and establish cause–effect relationships between characters or events, giving an insight into the child's cognitive development and the extent to which known developmental milestones have been reached (Liles, 1993).

When it comes to language education and narrative abilities, we are trained to think that some abilities develop uniquely in each language, which implies that they can be acquired – and above all tested – in isolation from other languages. Some abilities, however, are shared across languages and can be easily tested across languages, among which narrative abilities feature. They can be easily tested with multilinguals by analysing story grammar components (Stein & Glenn, 1975) such as the presence or absence in a story of a Setting and, within Episodes, of an Initial Event, an Internal Response, a Plan, an Attempt, a Consequence and a Reaction. The study discussed in Chapter 7 examines story grammar components across the three languages of instruction used in Ladin schools, focusing on the thresholds of language competence required to be able to engage in an age-appropriate narrative task.

6.1 Using Narratives in Linguistics and Education

In linguistics and education, narratives are employed for a wide range of purposes. First, they are widely recognised as excellent diagnostic tools for children with SLI (Botting, 2002) and are commonly used for this purpose in combination with other formal screening tools (Reese *et al.*, 2012). Monolingual and bilingual children with developmental language issues have difficulties recounting events and structuring simple narratives using logical and age-appropriate sequences. Narratives are considered particularly suitable for identifying these issues because children need to use age-appropriate linguistic and cognitive skills, including knowledge of social conventions, and display patterns of logical sequences and predictable structures with which children with SLI tend to struggle. Second, narratives are very useful to distinguish children with SLI from those whose difficulties are due to normal second language development. Poor academic performance is often attributed to the presence of language disorders in children, which is a common mistake to make with second language learners who have poor language skills in the language(s) of instruction rather than some kind of language impairment (Armon-Lotem *et al.*, 2015; Cummins, 1980, 1984; Meschi *et al.*, 2012; Samson & Lesaux, 2009; Sanchez *et al.*, 2013).

Recent research with bilingual children with and without SLI has mainly focused on production and, to a much lesser extent, on comprehension (Cleave *et al.*, 2010; Fiestas & Peña, 2004; Gutierrez-Clellen *et al.*, 2008; Iluz-Cohen & Walters, 2012; Pearson, 2002; Uccelli & Páez, 2007). A shared issue that has emerged from this work is the general lack of reliable instruments for the evaluation of bilingual narratives, which is due to a lack of normed instruments for bilingual assessment and a total lack of instruments for many of the world's languages (Gagarina *et al.*, 2012). It was this gap that led Gagarina *et al.* (2012) to create the Multilingual Assessment Instrument for Narratives (MAIN): a bilingual instrument for narratives designed to identify children with and without SLI using different language combinations. The MAIN and its application in bilingual narrative research are reviewed in Section 6.4.

Narratives are also regularly used in educational settings with TD children who speak one or more languages to monitor language development and identify possible areas of intervention and improvement. Narrative abilities are of special interest to educators because they are closely linked to literacy development and can serve to predict the child's degree of academic success during their school years (Heilmann *et al.*, 2010; Squires *et al.*, 2014). Bilingual children are exposed to narratives from an early age, depending on the type of bilingualism they are developing and the language choices their parents have made for them. The quality and quantity of input in both languages will ultimately determine the degree of bilingualism they develop and the level of maintenance required for both languages. Whether children are exposed to two languages from birth or begin to develop their bilingualism later in life, they usually begin to receive narrative input in at least one language when first exposed to picture books and short stories within the family and/or the childcare environment. They typically continue to develop their narrative skills up to school age and by that time have already developed the ability to establish causal and temporal links between characters and events and are able to tell stories using complete episodes. Narratives grow in depth and complexity as children grow older and are progressively able to understand, process and produce more elaborate input and more complex language. Narratives therefore offer a clear window on children's language development, providing valuable information to teachers who may adopt remedial strategies in the classroom whenever needed.

The South Tyrol study discussed in Chapter 7 provides an example of how narratives can be used in a multilingual educational programme where parallel language development is a fundamental educational goal for all students attending the programme. The study shows the kind of feedback that can be offered to teachers and educators and the value of monitoring progress and developing individualised remedial strategies for children with different language backgrounds. Since this study focused on narratives, this chapter is dedicated to reviewing the core literature on bilingual narratives, with special reference to the instruments that can be used for assessment in more than one language (Section 6.2) and the most common measures of narrative analysis (Sections 6.3 and 6.4).

6.2 Eliciting Narratives

There are different ways to elicit children's narratives in one or more languages. The most common methods are story generation/telling, story retelling and spontaneous speech production tasks, the difference between them based on presentation modality (visual or oral) and the cognitive demand that each task poses to the narrator.

Regarding presentation modality, stories can be presented orally or shown using pictures or videos. The suitability of each modality must be carefully evaluated with reference to the study design and the questions that are being asked, since the quality and quantity of narrative production are linked to both presentation modality (Schneider, 1996) and the type of task used (Roch *et al.*, 2016). The oral and visual modalities can be used separately or mixed, depending on the age of the children and whether participants are TD children or children with SLI.

Each task places different cognitive demands on the narrator who will engage in different processes when completing the task. A story that is presented orally places considerable demands on working memory, as the child needs to store enough information to repeat the story and must remember many details, such as the story setting, the characters' objectives, actions and feelings, the outcome of the story and the sequence of events. For young children and children with SLI, listening to content and remembering it with enough accuracy to repeat it can be very challenging, and the use of images is a common technique to avoid overloading the child's working memory with oral information. Whether the oral or visual mode is used, the use of stimuli provides the child with structured guidance that can be followed during the narrative.

Different elicitation materials can be used with children with and without SLI. Two of the most common stories are *The Bus Story* (Renfrew, 1969) and *Frog, Where Are You?* (Mayer, 1969). Renfrew's *The Bus Story* seems to be more common in research involving children with SLI (Cleave *et al.*, 2010) while the *Frog, Where Are You?* story can be found in a broader range of research where participants are children with or without SLI or are second language learners (Berman & Slobin, 1994; Fiestas & Peña, 2004; Gutierrez-Clellen *et al.*, 2008; Pearson, 2002). Other common elicitation materials include stories from the Edmonton Narrative Norms Instrument (ENNI) (see, i.e. Cleave *et al.*, 2010), a normed instrument developed at the University of Alberta, Canada, for 4- to 9-year-old children. The pictures for the ENNI were not borrowed from any known picture book or story but specifically designed by professional artists. The pictures vary in their level of difficulty: some show simple stories with two characters; others, complex stories with multiple characters (Schneider *et al.*, 2006).

While these elicitation materials are the most common, there is no hard and fast rule when it comes to choosing pictures for elicitation purposes, and several other options can be found in the literature. For example, in addition to the *Frog, Where Are You?* story, Gutierrez-Clellen *et al.* (2008) used another Mayer and Mayer (1975) story, *One Frog too Many*. Fiestas and Peña (2004), who work in the US context and more specifically in Texas, introduced a culturally relevant picture for their Spanish–English bilingual participants. The picture showed birthday party celebrations in a traditional Mexican family, with a piñata, a cake and several relatives in a yard enjoying the party. Iluz-Cohen and Walters (2012) opted for pictures of familiar stories like *The Jungle Book* and *Goldilocks and the Three Bears*.

The use of pictures to elicit narratives is particularly valuable with second language learners. Children who are going through the process of learning a second or additional language may find it difficult to understand a story without being able to refer to visual stimuli. They may be asked to retell a story, but if they do not understand it, they will never be able to repeat it. Pictures help the child focus on the content of the story without having to rely on oral information for comprehension. To overcome comprehension difficulties, videos can also be used without language or with minimal language input. Pictures also offer great potential for data comparison but also have some limitations. One advantage of using pictures is that researchers can compare their findings with those of research studies conducted in different contexts with children of similar or different ages or who speak other languages; a disadvantage is that results are limited to the story described and some aspects of language development may not fully emerge.

A great deal of narrative research has focused on identifying language impairments, so the emphasis has not been on TD immigrant or minority language speakers. Several studies have claimed that not all elicitation materials are equally effective and that the same children may behave differently when using different elicitation materials. These claims come from different studies. Westerveld and Vidler (2015), for instance, wanted to determine which elicitation material between the frequently used *Frog, Where Are You?* story (Mayer, 1969) and *The Bus Story* (Renfrew, 1969) yielded the best results with school-age children with SLI. They compared the narratives generated by the two stories and showed that language impairments were being overidentified with *The Bus Story*, with 21%–64% of children achieving substandard results in terms of information and length, while, when the *Frog, Where are You?* story was used, the children were able to produce longer samples and a more varied vocabulary. Other studies, however, found *The Bus Story* to be very effective, with reported rates of 84% of children correctly identified as having language impairments (Pankratz *et al.*, 2007). Asking similar questions, Schneider *et al.* (2006) focused on the effectiveness of the ENNI and one measure of narrative ability: the story grammar unit (SGU). The authors were interested in establishing whether the ENNI could capture language development and, above all, successfully distinguish between children with and without language impairments. They tested 377 children, aged 4–9 years, 77 of whom had language impairments and the rest were TD children. They found the ENNI to be highly effective as almost 80.8% of the children tested were correctly identified as having language impairments.

Even though this volume is not directly concerned with the identification of language impairments, these studies are relevant to a volume on multilingual testing and assessment as they convey the shared message that the quality and quantity of output can be affected when using different materials with the same children – and probably even more so when the children are non-native speakers of the language of testing. As we will see in Chapter 7, one of the questions raised by the South Tyrol study is related to the level of language competence required for immigrant children to perform in a narrative task with results similar to those of children of the same age but of different language backgrounds. In light of the evidence that different stimuli may lead to differences in output, the study used two silent videos, providing children with the opportunity to structure the stories without further visual input. This will be discussed in more detail in Chapter 7.

6.3 Measures of Narrative Analysis

The most used measures of narrative analysis are measures of microstructure and macrostructure, which represent two distinct aspects of narrative competence and underlying narrative abilities (Liles *et al.*, 1995). Macrostructure focuses on narrative structure, and microstructure, on language and grammar. Measures of macrostructure and microstructure may vary from one study to another, depending on researchers' interest or focus, while some measures have been shown by comparative studies (Heilmann *et al.*, 2010) to be more effective than others.

6.3.1 Macrostructure

Narrative macrostructure captures the internal structure of a story, also commonly known as story grammar (Stein & Glenn, 1975). It focuses on the higher-order categories involved in the analysis, creation and evaluation of content and reflects the way narrative content is organised within the story. Macrostructure is typically measured by observing the presence or absence of a certain number of components within the story, from information on the Setting to some or all of the following elements within an Episode: an Initiating Event, an Internal Response, a Plan, an Attempt, a Consequence and a Reaction.

The main components of a narrative structure are the Setting and the Episode. The Setting includes information about the time and place of the story and the main characters. Episodes can be more than one and include the components listed above. The Initiating Event provides information about the event that represents a problem for the main character(s) and that needs to be solved, which could be an external or internal event, such as a thought or a desire. The Internal Response describes the reaction of the main character(s) to the Initiating Event. The Plan explains what the main character(s) intend to do to solve the problem, and one or more Attempts can be made to solve it. The Consequence of the Attempt(s) could be a success or a failure, to which a final Reaction provides details of the main character(s) response.

Measures of macrostructure and scoring criteria can vary from one study to another, as different emphasis may be placed on different components. All stories are believed to have a Setting and one or more Episodes, so these are the elements that all studies focus on. A specific research study may then focus on different details within each Episode, which leads to the creation and use of different scoring rubrics. Pearson (2002: 141), for instance, examined internal structure by using what she refers to as a 'Story Score': a scoring rubric described as a set of measures designed to evaluate 'the child's ability to use a hierarchical story structure, maintain a clear flow of information, and include evaluative and metacognitive statements in recounting the events'. The 'Story Score' can be broken down into five core elements: Story Elements, Sequencing, Reference to the story's characters, Reference to Internal States and Engagement. The same scoring criteria were used for assessment in Uccelli and Páez (2007). A different focus is found in the MAIN (Gagarina *et al.*, 2012), which examines internal structure by focusing on story structure components (goal, attempt and outcome sequences), structural complexity (goal-directed behaviour) and internal states (mental states terms). The South Tyrol study reviewed in Chapter 7 instead focused on goal, attempt and outcome sequences, as well as goal-directed behaviour. Despite the slight differences in focus between one study and another, all measures of macrostructure are designed to break down internal structure components and identify the core elements of narrative structure.

The study of macrostructure has attracted the attention of scholars working in education because of its potential use in the classroom context. There is a clear association between macrostructure, literacy development and academic progress (Heilmann *et al.*, 2010; Squires *et al.*, 2014) and pre-primary macrostructure scores are known to predict children's narrative abilities in primary school (Squires *et al.*, 2014). Teachers who work with narratives often use pedagogical strategies based on macrostructure that involve techniques that can help children focus on content and develop the details of a story (e.g. What does the bunny do? How is the girl feeling? What happens next?). Questioning techniques have proved very useful in developing children's narrative skills (Lever & Sénéchal, 2011), showing the valuable role of interaction throughout the learning process, which is also considered essential in promoting second language development in children and adults.

All narratives are believed to share a fundamentally similar structure organised around one or more goal–attempt–outcome sequences of the main character(s) (Trabasso & Nickels, 1992). The claim of macrostructure stability between languages comes from research on bilingual narratives (Altman *et al.*, 2016; Hipfner-Boucher *et al.*, 2014; Iluz-Cohen & Walters, 2012; Pearson, 2002; Uccelli & Páez, 2007), where stability is also taken to be evidence that bilingualism does not pose a disadvantage to bilingual language development (Hipfner-Boucher *et al.*, 2014; Pearson, 2002). As is often the case with research involving speakers of more than one language, the information available does not go beyond bilingualism and bilingual narratives. Very little is currently known about the mechanisms underlying the development of narrative skills in more than two languages, so it is not yet possible to say whether the same claim of stability can be extended to multilingual speakers.

6.3.2 Macrostructure stability and language proficiency

The claim that macrostructure remains stable across more than two languages is reviewed in this section, as the South Tyrol study specifically examines the role of language proficiency in relation to macrostructure stability and the identification of threshold levels in students' languages.

A question about macrostructure stability is also a question about transfer and how transfer operates across languages. Transfer, or crosslinguistic influence, is traditionally conceived as a process in which some elements or features of a language are transferred into one or more languages. When three or more languages are learned simultaneously, however, it may be inappropriate to refer to a transfer process, as elements of narrative macrostructure may be more simply shared among languages as a result of acquisition rather than transfer. This would not be the case for an immigrant child who is familiar with narrative macrostructure in his/her native language, for instance, and who transfers elements of macrostructure into the language(s) of instruction the child is learning as his/her command of these languages grows.

A claim of macrostructure stability implies that one is able to identify if the macrostructure is stable, when it stabilises, the role of language proficiency in each of the multilinguals' languages and what may be transferred between language systems, i.e. whether all elements of macrostructure transfer equally across languages. One may also want to explore whether significant differences arise when multilinguals develop their language knowledge simultaneously or consecutively.

Regarding macrostructure stability when multiple languages are known, to the best of my knowledge there is no published research on narratives in more than two languages, so we can only make assumptions based on the information currently available. While it seems reasonable to assume that stability between languages will hold – as has already been shown to happen with bilinguals – the presence of more than two languages in the mind raises further concerns about the amount of knowledge needed for transfer to occur, with the possibility that the transfer of elements of macrostructure will emerge in some but not all languages, depending on the level of proficiency achieved.

Before the child can produce a coherent story with episodes and goal–attempt–outcome sequences, it is reasonable to assume that a minimal level of language knowledge must be reached, or production would not be possible or too fragmented to be sufficiently comprehensible. Individual variability is a well-known problem for assessment and even more so with multilinguals whose proficiency level in their languages is likely to differ and fluctuate widely from person to person. Multilinguals are rarely a homogeneous group. They have language backgrounds that differ in the type and number of languages known and in the level of competence achieved in each language. The question of when macrostructure may stabilise across languages is therefore essentially a question about the role of language proficiency and the amount of language knowledge required for transfer to occur. Research on low proficiency background languages indicates that even a few years of exposure to a language is sufficient to show significant differences in production and influence the acquisition of additional languages (Bardel & Lindqvist, 2007; De Angelis, 2007, 2018; Rast, 2010). The possibility that transfer will occur in conjunction with low levels of proficiency is therefore reasonable and worth investigating but needs to be explored further, while threshold levels remain to be identified.

With regard to the question of whether all elements of macrostructure transfer equally across languages, it would also be relevant to establish whether threshold levels can be identified for each language and whether elements of macrostructure transfer once a threshold is reached or at different times during the language developmental process. I will return to a discussion of the role of language proficiency and threshold levels in relation to macrostructure in Chapter 7.

6.3.3 Microstructure

The second measure of narrative analysis focuses on microstructure and the language used in the narration. Through a series of productivity indices, measures of microstructure evaluate the frequency of appearance of different elements that are used to determine lexical and grammatical complexity, fluency, internal cohesion, pragmatic knowledge and so forth. Microstructure is language-specific so it cannot be easily separated from the language of narration or the narrator's level of proficiency in that language. As was the case with macrostructure, the evidence that is currently available comes from research with bilinguals rather than multilinguals. There is, however, research on cross-linguistic influence and multilingual speakers that draws on similar productivity indices and can offer useful information for narrative research.

Measures of microstructure vary from study to study and, since they are based on frequency of occurrence, the range of possibilities is extremely broad. Any element of grammar that can be counted can be used for the analysis of narrative microstructure. Justice et al. (2006) provide a good summary of microstructure indices suitable for clinical purposes with school-age children. A good example of microstructure indices in bilingual narrative research is the selection used in the MAIN (Gagarina et al., 2012). The measures chosen for analysis focus on narrative length and lexis (total number of tokens, number of different words used within each category, number of communication units), morphosyntactic complexity, discourse cohesion (mean length of communication units) and syntactic complexity (verb clauses, subordination, coordination).

Measures of microstructure have been generally found to be robust predictors of language development (Wolfe-Quintero et al., 1998). Type-token ratios (TTRs) are often used for analysis in lexical research, even though they have also attracted a good deal of criticism because their reliability is argued to depend on text length (Crossley et al., 2011; Lissón & Ballier, 2018). TTRs are based on a very simple formula that divides the different types produced – for example, nouns – by the total number of tokens (overall number of nouns) produced.

In contrast to the widespread claim of stability for macrostructures, past research has found microstructure to be highly unstable between language systems, with a notable difference between the narratives produced by TD children and by children with SLI. TD children show narrative microstructure with significant differences across languages, while children with SLI show a much narrower divergence (Altman et al., 2016; Cleave et al., 2010; Fiestas & Peña, 2004; Gutierrez-Clellen et al., 2008; Hipfner-Boucher et al., 2014; Iluz-Cohen & Walters, 2012; Pearson, 2002; Uccelli & Páez, 2007). Evidence of this kind suggests different patterns of language development in children with language impairments (Cleave et al., 2010) and consequently a different impact of bilingualism on language development.

As it is quantitative in nature, microstructure analysis is particularly suitable for computer analysis. A software widely used for this purpose (see Cleave et al., 2010; Fiestas & Peña, 2004; Gutierrez-Clellen et al., 2008) is the Systematic Analysis of Language Transcripts (SALT) software (https://www.saltsoftware.com/products/elicitation-materials). Making use of the Narrative Scoring Scheme (NNS) developed at the University of Wisconsin, SALT is a very useful software package capable of analysing both macrostructure and microstructure, but its use is limited to specific populations as it is only available in English and Spanish.

Hence, its main limitation is that it cannot be used with multilinguals or bilinguals who have knowledge of other languages.

6.4 The Multilingual Assessment Instrument for Narratives

The MAIN (Gagarina *et al.*, 2012) is a tool designed for the assessment of narratives produced by bilingual children aged 3–10 years. It was developed in recent years within the framework of the European Cooperation in Science and Technology (COST) Action ISO804 Language Impairment in a Multilingual Society: Linguistic Patterns and the Road to Assessment and is part of the Language Impairment Testing in Multilingual Settings (LITMUS) battery of tests.

The MAIN was created to provide a reliable tool that would allow researchers, practitioners and educators working in different contexts to identify bilingual children with SLI. The wider goal was to devise an instrument that would be appropriate for children with different language and cultural backgrounds and for children with and without SLI. The 'Narrative and Discourse' group working within COST Action ISO804 initially intended to evaluate existing narrative elicitation tools and their suitability for bilingual populations with language impairments. Following this initial review phase, the group concluded that what was available was insufficient or inadequate, so they decided to develop an entirely new evaluation tool for assessment: the MAIN (Gagarina *et al.*, 2012). The MAIN has been tested with more than 500 children using 15 different language pairs and is now available in more than 30 languages (Gagarina *et al.*, 2012). Despite its name, however, the tool has only been used with bilingual children.

The MAIN is organised into different components and can be used with different types of narrative tasks, such as story generation/telling a story, telling a story (after listening to it) or retelling a story (after hearing an entirely different but structurally similar story). Its main feature is that it contains parallel stories called *Baby Birds*, *Baby Goats*, *Dog* and *Cat*, and each story is built using a sequence of six pictures. A script is provided for each story, together with scoring instructions and some open-ended questions aimed at identifying objectives and internal states. A questionnaire for parents or caregivers is also included, which is designed to elicit personal background information about the child, including age, prior attendance at kindergarten or school, country of birth and any evidence of hearing or speech difficulties. Further questions focus on parental background information, the languages of communication between parents and siblings in the home environment, the estimated amount of input in each language and the level of competence achieved. The levels of literacy-related activities are also examined, such as the frequency with which the child reads books, tells stories, listens to songs, sings and watches media of various kinds.

The MAIN rests on the assumption that narrative assessment must include both macrostructure and microstructure components in order to be effective. As reviewed earlier in the chapter, macrostructure refers to the internal structure of the story while microstructure refers to the language used in the narration, which is measured using productivity indices. Regarding macrostructure, the MAIN uses three main measures: (i) story structure components, (ii) structural complexity and (iii) internal states. The first measure of story structure components is based on predetermined sequences. Each of the four stories – *Baby Birds*, *Baby Goats*, *Dog* and *Cat* – includes three episodes which share the same number of Goal, Attempt and Outcome sequences. The Goal refers to what the characters intend to do in response to the problem outlined in the Initiating Event, and different characters may set different goals; the Attempt refers to what the characters do to achieve what is set out in the Goal; and the Outcome refers to the consequence of the Attempt. The story ends when the Goal is finally achieved. The second measure of structural complexity – based on Westby (2005) – assesses the presence or absence of information about goal-directed behaviour that determines whether an episode is simple, complete or incomplete. Its focus is on whether there is a simple sequence without a specified Goal; a simple episode with a Goal but no Attempt or Outcome; or a complete episode with a Goal, an Attempt and an Outcome. The third measure is the newest of all and refers to mental state terms that are believed to offer a window on the child's interpretation of the characters' actions. Two internal state terms are part of each episode, so the three episodes of a story include a total of 15 components (9 goal–attempt–outcome sequences and 6 internal state terms).

Measures of microstructure are organised into three main groups: (i) narrative length and lexis, (ii) morphosyntactic complexity and discourse cohesion and (iii) syntactic complexity. A range of quantitative indexes are used for measurements. Measures of narrative length and lexis include the total number of tokens, the number of different words used and the number of communication units. Measures of morphosyntactic complexity and discourse cohesion include the mean length of the three main communication units, while syntactic complexity uses the number of verb clauses, the ratio of verb clauses and the amount of subordination and coordination.

Overall, the MAIN is now widely regarded as a useful narrative assessment tool offering several advantages for research purposes. Firstly, the MAIN is language independent, so it can be easily used with different language combinations. This language independence feature makes it a highly versatile tool, particularly for macrostructure analysis. Secondly, it has already been used with a number of language combinations, so that the use of the same materials and the same frameworks with different languages makes cross-language comparability one of its main strengths. Thirdly, its use increased general awareness of the issues surrounding bilingual narrative assessment in the field.

The MAIN was developed within the story grammar theoretical framework (Stein & Glenn, 1975), which was, in turn, strongly influenced by another model proposed around the same time by Rumelhart (1975). Rumelhart's research had mainly focused on oral narratives, a form of exposition that can be subject to a great deal of variation when the story is repeated several times. Despite the great variability and the inevitable changes within storylines, Rumelhart had initially identified features of stability within the internal organisational structure, the logical sequence of components and the hierarchical binary relationship between the components. Stein and Glenn (1975) later expanded on Rumelhart's original model because, when they tried to apply it to children's literature, they found it insufficiently developed to capture the internal story structure. Stein and Glenn (1975) then proposed that all stories include two main components: a Setting and one or more Episodes. The Setting provides information about the time and location of the story and the main characters; and the Episode includes a number of components, such as an Initiating Event, an Internal Response, a Plan, an Attempt, a Consequence and a Reaction, all of which are causally or temporally linked to the main characters.

6.5 Assessing Multilingual Narratives and the South Tyrol Study

Narrative research has made great progress since the 1970s, identifying distinctive patterns and components of internal story grammar in both monolingual and bilingual narratives. Despite the importance of narrative research, however, there is still very little evidence for how narrative abilities develop in multiple language speakers with or without SLI, which is a significant theoretical void in the field and for those interested in the use of narratives in education. Very little is known about the role of language dominance in supporting the development of narrative abilities, unless it is the dominance of the mother tongue, and about the role of language competence in individual languages, the association between quality and quantity of input and the development of narrative abilities in different languages.

In multilingual educational contexts, questions about language, language dominance and language proficiency are central to scholarly discussions about teaching, learning and assessment. Poor language skills are often perceived to be one of the main obstacles to learning and to fair testing practices. For this reason, when testing linguistically and culturally diverse student populations, it is good practice to focus on knowledge that allows students not to be heavily reliant on language proficiency. Story grammars represent this kind of knowledge, which is one of the main reasons for choosing to use story grammars and narratives for assessment purposes in the complex multilingual contexts of South Tyrol, Italy.

7 Multilingual Narratives: The South Tyrol Study

The South Tyrol study is a 2-year longitudinal research project conducted between 2014 and 2016 in collaboration with the Ladin school board of the Province of Bolzano-Bolzen, Italy. The overall project included four data collections, approximately one every 6 months. The first and second data collection elicited narratives using picture description tasks, the third asked participants to produce free narratives and the fourth used two Disney Pixar short silent films. The data was analysed using a combination of qualitative and quantitative analysis techniques. Of relevance to this volume is the fourth data collection, which focused on the use of multilingual narratives for formative assessment purposes. The aim of the three previous data collections was to identify how best to monitor language development over the 2-year period and longer periods of time, in addition to examining the interaction between the students' languages. The first three data collections, in other words, were not developed with formative assessment in mind and for this reason have not been included in this chapter.

The chapter is organised as follows. Following a description of the unique multilingual context of South Tyrol (Section 7.1), the chapter presents the study's research aims and questions (Section 7.2) and gives an overview of immigration to the region, including the number of children attending local Ladin schools (Section 7.3). This is followed by the study methodology (Section 7.4), results (Section 7.5) and discussion (Section 7.6).

7.1 The Multilingual Context of South Tyrol

The study was conducted in the valleys of the Province of Bolzano-Bolzen which, together with the Province of Trento, form the Trentino-Alto Adige/Südtirol region. According to the latest available national census figures, in 2011 the Province of Bolzano-Bolzen had a population of 504,643 inhabitants, an increase of 9% compared to the 2001 census, when the number of inhabitants recorded was 462,999 (ASTAT, n.d.).

South Tyrol is a small area of 7400 sq. km (2857 sq. miles) and is home to people of different ethnic groups who speak different native languages. German, Italian and Ladin represent the three main language groups. According to the 2011 census, the Italian-speaking population is 26.06%, the German-speaking population is 69.41% and the Ladin-speaking population is 4.53%. The immigrant population is also steadily growing, and many immigrant children now live in the region and attend local schools.

Ladin is a Romance language spoken in five of the Dolomites valleys of northern Italy. Two of these valleys are located in the Province of Bolzano-Bolzen (Val Gardena/Gherdëina and Val Badia) where the South Tyrol study took place. Some data was also collected in a third valley (Val di Fassa/Fascia) located in the neighbouring Province of Trento. The remaining two valleys are in the Province of Belluno in the neighbouring Veneto region, but no data was collected in these areas.

The presence of the Ladin and German language groups in the Alto Adige/Südtirol region is secular, while the Italian language group is part of a more recent and complex history. South Tyrol became part of Italy immediately after the First World War, when under fascist rule a series of educational and economic measures were introduced to attract Italians to live and work in the region. In the 1930s, German speakers were the largest ethnic group in the area. With the objective of weakening their status, measures were introduced to replace German with Italian. The use of German was abolished in schools, public offices and all other public services. In 1939, those who did not accept the Italianisation of the region were given the opportunity to move to other German-speaking areas outside of the country. Many left but after the Second World War decided to return, to find a deeply changed land.

The local population was unhappy mainly because the newly formed Italian government did not offer sufficient protection to the minorities living in the area. Extensive negotiations took place that eventually succeeded in providing legislative protection for Ladin and German speakers in the region (Eichinger, 2010; Van der Schaaf & Verra, 2001). The first Statute of Autonomy of 1948, which offered little protection, was subsequently revised and a second statute, which finally offered the increased protection the population of South Tyrol was looking for, was approved in 1972. As part of the measures introduced by the Italian government, all language groups were given the right to education in their mother tongue – a decision that led to the establishment of three distinct school boards: the Italian school board, the German school board and the Ladin school board. These three school boards are still operational and continue to oversee teaching in the area. By statute, the German and Italian school boards have adopted a teaching model that includes the first language (L1) (German or Italian) used to teach all subjects and the compulsory teaching of the other language as a second language (L2) (German or Italian). Ladin schools instead follow a multilingual educational model where subjects are taught in German and Italian, while Ladin is used as a language of communication and is also taught as a subject. This agreement was set out in the 1972 Statute of Autonomy's Article 19, which reads as follows:

> In the Province of Bolzano nursery, primary and secondary school teaching shall be provided in the Italian or German mother-tongue of the pupils by teachers of the same mother-tongue. In primary schools, beginning with the second or third year, to be established by provincial law on the binding proposal of the linguistic group concerned, and in secondary schools, the teaching of the second language by teachers for whom it is their mother-tongue shall be compulsory. The Ladin language shall be used in nursery schools and shall be taught in primary schools in Ladin areas. Ladin shall also be used as a teaching language in schools of every type and grade in those areas. In such schools teaching shall be given on the basis of the same number of hours and the same level in Italian and German [...] (Woodcock, 1992: 139–140)

Successful multilingual teaching requires a qualified multilingual workforce. The Ladin school board currently employs approximately 400 trilingual (Ladin, German, Italian) teachers who are required to take a trilingual exam to enter the public education system. Primary schoolteachers receive educational training in the three languages of instruction at the trilingual University of Bolzano-Bozen, where a dedicated teacher training programme has been set up to meet the requirements of the local multilingual workforce.

7.2 Research Aims and Questions

Several educational and research objectives guided the South Tyrol project, whose overarching aim was to assess multilingual students' learning progress during the school year and obtain information that would be useful for teachers, students and their families. The project was implemented because the Ladin school board wanted to provide a good educational experience for the immigrant children entering the education system with limited knowledge of the three languages of instruction (Italian, German and Ladin), while also maintaining high educational standards for local Ladin children already attending local schools and ensuring their learning needs continued to be fully met.

Many of the immigrant children attending Ladin schools speak home languages that differ from the three languages of instruction, so between the home language practices and the school language requirements, children starting the primary school cycle are typically required to function in at least four languages, with the introduction of English as an additional language in fourth year. For teachers and principals working with these children, a natural question is whether immigrant children can effectively deal with so many languages from an early age or whether it would be better to introduce them to the languages of instruction more gradually. School staff are also concerned about children's overall school performance, as poor knowledge of the languages of instruction is often perceived to be a major obstacle to their learning progress.

In addition to these educational goals, the study was also guided by the broader aim of understanding how to test multilingual children in contexts where multilingual speakers may not only be immigrant students but also, and above all, students who grow up speaking different languages in the family and social context. The wider goal was therefore to go beyond bilingualism and bilingual assessment research and explore testing options suitable for multilingual speakers with very different backgrounds, experiences and profiles. The intention was to gather information that could be used for a variety of formative purposes, ranging from in-service teacher training to classroom feedback and materials development. Multilingual narratives were considered the most suitable to meet these goals because Ladin schools already adopt multilingual strategies in teaching narratives to children. With an integrated approach to language education, reading materials are typically presented and summarised using the three languages of instruction and all activities involve the use of the three languages. During in-class reading activities, for instance, a text may be read in German, a comprehension question may be asked in Italian and an answer may be required in Ladin. The use of languages is fluid and flexible, and boundaries are not as strict as they would be in mainstream monolingual education. Examples of these activities can be viewed at Ciamp Pedagogich (http://www.pedagogich.it/unites_it.html). On the website, activities are available in Ladin, German and Italian, but the reader can easily translate the explanatory text into English. One pedagogical feature I would like to draw attention to is the use of the same colour for each of the languages used in the school. These colours are used both for teaching and on posters displayed in class and throughout the school: green stands for Ladin, red for German and yellow for Italian.

Chapter 6 examined bilingual narrative research and discussed how most of what we know about the development of narrative abilities in multiple languages remains limited to bilingualism and to children with or without specific language impairment (SLI). The literature on narratives is in itself quite extensive – especially research on bilingual children with SLI – and has not only some important strengths but also some weaknesses. The main strengths are undoubtedly the wealth of information on children with and without SLI and the range of language combinations examined over the years; the main weaknesses relate to the lack of information on narrative abilities beyond two languages, including evidence of the role of language proficiency in fostering or hindering language development. These weaknesses represent a critical challenge for the field of multilingual testing and assessment as the role of language proficiency has only been considered in relation to bilingualism to date. The study of South Tyrol thus begins to fill this theoretical void by exploring the association between the development of narrative abilities across three languages and the role that language proficiency plays in the developmental process.

In Chapter 6, I discussed how all stories are believed to have an internal episode structure that is universal and stable across language systems (Altman *et al.*, 2016; Hipfner-Boucher *et al.*, 2014; Iluz-Cohen & Walters, 2012; Pearson, 2002; Uccelli & Páez, 2007), which is why macrostructure is believed to easily transfer between languages. Other studies, however, suggest that macrostructure stability depends on the level of language proficiency the speaker achieves in his/her languages (Gutiérrez-Clellen, 2002; Montanari, 2004). This is a possibility that is essential to explore with multiple language speakers, especially since language proficiency in background languages tends to fluctuate over short periods of time. In contrast, microstructure appears to be highly unstable between language systems and this is generally considered as evidence that transfer does not occur at the microstructural level.

The evidence for macrostructure stability comes from research with bilingual participants and from narrative samples produced in two languages. To the best of my knowledge, no research is available on narratives produced in more than two languages that can provide additional input in relation to macrostructure stability and language proficiency across multiple languages. The South Tyrol study aimed to provide additional information on macrostructure stability across a minimum of three languages and examine whether cross-linguistic influence is indeed the underlying process that facilitates overt stability. To this end, the study addressed the following research questions: (1) Do multilingual children's narratives vary between three languages with regard to macrostructure? (2) Do multilingual children perform differently at different proficiency levels? (3) Can a threshold level be identified for cross-linguistic influence to arise in relation to macrostructure?

These questions were addressed by gathering information about learners' proficiency levels in the three languages of instruction through the collection of an oral narrative sample in each language. As we shall see, obtaining data for each individual language does not necessarily translate into a monolingual approach to assessment, particularly as in this case the focus was on underlying narrative abilities common to all languages. The object of the evaluation was, in other words, narrative abilities, not the language in which these abilities were expressed. This point will become clearer in the results and discussion sections of the reported study.

7.3 Immigrant Population in South Tyrol and Ladin Schools

South Tyrol's immigrant population has been growing steadily and has more than quadrupled in 20 years. According to the Provincial Institute of Statistics (ASTAT, n.d.), in 2018 there were 50,333 foreign nationals formally resident in the Province of Bolzano-Bolzen – an increase of 4.8% from 2017. Twenty years earlier, in 1998, there had been only 11,600. Immigrants come from several different countries and continents (see Figure 7.1) and those who have reached South Tyrol over the past 25 years are mostly first-generation immigrants.

According to ASTAT (n.d.), the immigrant population is also very young. The mean age is 35.4, about 60% of whom are younger than 40. In contrast, the older immigrant population (over 65) is quite small (6.1%) in comparison to the number of seniors among the local population (21%). The typical immigrant profile in South Tyrol is therefore that of young men and women whose children attend local schools. Table 7.1 provides descriptive enrolment statistics for immigrant children attending Ladin schools in the Gherdëina and Badia Valleys.

As mentioned at the beginning of the chapter, the constant flow of students with a migratory background and the need for them to learn and master three languages to successfully complete the trilingual school cycle initially motivated the Ladin school board to identify best practices for schools, teachers and children. The Ladin school board expressed an interest in understanding how long it would take children with such a background to reach the level of native peers considering the complexity of the South Tyrol context and the different language practices used

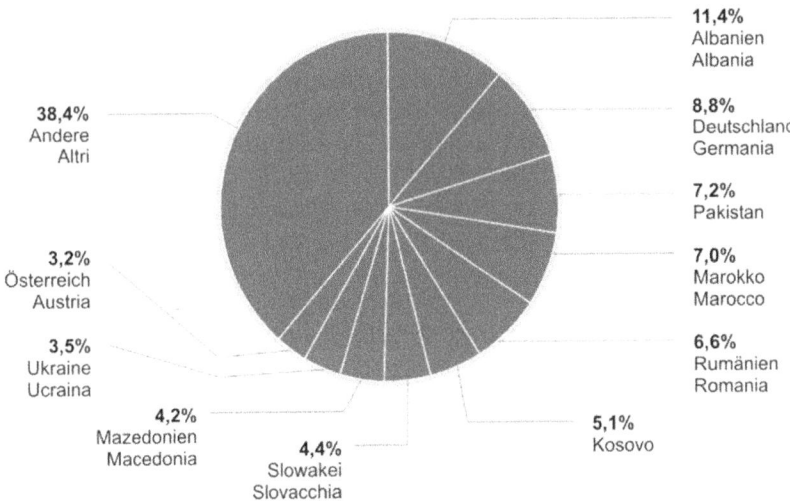

Figure 7.1 Province of Bolzano-Bozen: Foreign residents by nationality, 2018 (Source: ASTAT, n.d.)

Table 7.1 Immigrant children attending Ladin schools in the Gherdëina and Badia Valleys and total school population in 2018

School	Badia Valley	Total	%	Gherdëina Valley	Total	%
Kindergarten	21	368	5.71	37	356	10.39
Primary	19	597	3.18	53	545	9.72
Lower secondary	10	399	2.51	31	383	8.09
Upper secondary	0	117	0.00	11	403	2.73
Total	50	1478	3.38	132	1778	7.42

Source: Ladin school board.

in the region. The question the board asked is not new and has, in fact, been raised several times by various education boards and ministries of education over the years. The reason this question continues to be asked is that research in one sociolinguistic context is not necessarily generalisable to another, and only a careful assessment of local circumstances can give reliable context-specific information that can inform decisions for language policy and planning purposes.

A number of factors determine how well and how quickly children learn third or additional languages, including – but not limited to – the level of literacy in the L1, the languages spoken in the family and/or the community context, the quality and quantity of input in each language, the type and number of background languages already known and the typological or psychotypological distance between them. All these factors can influence the speed and rate of language development and can potentially inform the decision as to how early to introduce languages at school and whether sequential or simultaneous exposure is more appropriate for the child's age.

As past research has already shown (see Section 3.6), the average time for immigrant children to reach native peers varies considerably and largely depends on literacy in the L1 and the distance between languages. Children with literacy in the mother tongue usually take 5–7 years to reach native peers, while those without literacy or formal education in the L1 may take 7–9 years (Hakuta et al., 2000; Shohamy, 2011; Thomas & Collier, 2002). Shohamy (2011) showed that even longer periods of time apply when the typological distance between languages is greater. According to Shohamy, it can take Russian children 9–11 years to catch up with Hebrew monolinguals, while some Ethiopians are never able to reach them.

In light of this information, it is easy to understand why a careful evaluation of local circumstances in South Tyrol is fully warranted, particularly as several languages are spoken both by the immigrant community and within the community where Ladin schools are located, and Ladin, German and Italian are not equally distributed across valleys.

7.4 Methods

7.4.1 Participants and languages examined

Participants were from Ladin schools located in the Gherdëina and Badia Valleys of South Tyrol, and a small sample was from Ladin schools of the neighbouring Fassa/Fascia Valley of Trentino. Some immigrant children attending Italian and German schools in South Tyrol were also included for comparison purposes. All the participants were children and young teenagers from 6 to 13/14 years of age. Some were native speakers of Ladin with German and Italian as additional languages, while the rest were first- or second-generation immigrants with a range of different native languages: Albanian, Arabic, Bengali (Bangla), Macedonian, Malagasy, Moldavian, Punjabi, Romanian, Serbian, Ukrainian and Urdu.

Since the study was intended to be representative of the immigrant population of South Tyrol, which comes from all over the world (see Figure 7.1), no group of speakers with the same native language was singled out. Participants were examined in different languages, depending on school type, as summarised in Table 7.2.

The 15 Ladin L1 students were all born and raised in the region of South Tyrol, while the age of arrival of the immigrant children differed, as illustrated in Table 7.3. Most of the immigrants attending Ladin, Italian and German schools in South Tyrol were either born in Italy or had reached Italy at a very young age. The Ladin schools in the Fassa/Fascia Valley were the only schools where all the immigrant children were born outside of Italy, but most of them had reached the country at a very young age. A breakdown of individual ages of arrival by school and location is provided in Table 7.3.

7.4.2 Materials and procedures

The materials selected for the study were deliberately simple to use and the measures easy to understand for those who are non-linguists. It may be recalled that narratives were chosen for formative assessment purposes with the intention of showing teachers how to analyse narratives in multiple languages and draw inferences from the data that would be relevant to their particular sociolinguistic context. Teachers' independence was, in other words, one of the expected outcomes of this work.

Table 7.2 Participants and languages examined

School	Participants	Language(s) of assessment
Ladin (South Tyrol)	15 migrants 15 Ladin L1	Ladin, German, Italian
German (South Tyrol)	8 migrants	German
Italian (South Tyrol)	9 migrants	Italian
Ladin (Fassa/Fascia Valley)	9 migrants	Ladin and Italian

Table 7.3 Immigrants' age of arrival by school and location (South Tyrol or Fassa/Fascia)

AoA	Ladin, ST	Italian, ST	German, ST	Ladin Fassa/Fascia
0	7	4	5	0
1	1	0	0	0
2	1	0	0	1
3	0	0	0	1
4	1	1	1	1
5	0	0	1	3
6	0	1	1	1
7	1	1	0	0
8	1	1	0	0
9	1	0	0	0
10	1	0	0	0
13	1	1	0	0
Unknown	0	0	0	2
Total	15	9	8	9

Different types of materials were used in the study. Narratives were elicited using two Disney Pixar short movies, while background information from parents or guardians was obtained through a parental questionnaire and the assistance of the Ladin school board. Teachers also participated in professional development sessions throughout the 2-year period, which were attended by school principals as well.

Elicitation materials: Disney Pixar Movies

All participants were asked to watch two silent Disney Pixar movies freely available on YouTube: *La Luna* [Eng.: *The Moon*] and *Il regalo* [Eng.: *The Present*]. The first movie – *The Moon* – is a short film (6 minutes, 58 seconds) without dialogue. The second – *The Present*– is another short movie (4 minutes, 18 seconds) with minimal dialogue but was shown to participants without dialogue or subtitles. These two short movies were chosen for several reasons. First, the movies were either silent (*The Moon*) or suitable to be shown without dialogue or subtitles (*The Present*). Second, both movies were short enough for children to watch without losing concentration. Third, the movies showed a complete story that could be easily understood and summarised by children of any age. Fourth, the lack of verbal input allowed children with poor language proficiency to focus on the story rather than the language in which the story was told, eliminating the potential for comprehension problems. This last feature was, in fact, central to the decision to use videos instead of other types of elicitation materials. The two movies were thus deemed suitable for a linguistically and culturally diverse student population as they offered the advantage of not having to be linguistically simplified and the content did not contain any significant cultural bias.

After watching the two movies, participants were asked to summarise the episodes in individual languages (German, Ladin and Italian) and all narratives were recorded and transcribed. No specific order of preference was given, so this was completely random. One concern with this procedure was the possibility that repetition would generate a significant bias in the data collection. While past research found no significant bias in narrative repetition (Pearson, 2002), the possibility of a repetition bias was considered, so the data was subsequently examined to see whether a bias could be detected. Results clearly showed a difference in narrative patterns between Ladin L1 speakers and children with an immigrant background, which was taken to be evidence of no significant bias in the data collection procedure, as a bias cannot be language-selective and affect one group of speakers but not another. This can be viewed in more detail in Sections 7.5 and 7.6.

A second issue concerned the optimal amount of narrative structure that the children had to have in order to complete the narrative task as planned. Narratives can be elicited by giving different amounts of information to the narrator; the smaller the amount of information provided, the more difficult it is for the child to complete the task (Hutson-Nechkash, 1990). Silent movies provide a high degree of narrative structure to children and, in addition to helping overcome potential comprehension difficulties, they also offer the advantage of not providing language-specific input which could be a source of potential bias.

Parental questionnaire

A parental questionnaire was used to gather background information on the family's socioeconomic status (level of education, income and profession), home reading habits and estimated amount of input in each language. Some background information was also provided by the Ladin school board as they already knew the families of the children who participated in the study. The questionnaire was a slightly modified version of the parental questionnaire used in the PISA 2012 assessment exercise, which is freely available on the Organisation for Economic Co-Operation and Development (OECD) website (www.oecd.org).

7.4.3 Measures

Language proficiency

Language proficiency in the three languages of instruction (Ladin, German and Italian) was assessed by native speakers using the Common

European Framework of Reference for Languages (CEFR) descriptors for young learners available in the *Collated Representative Samples of Language Competences Developed for Young Learners aged 7–10 years* (Resource for Educators, Volume 1) and *11–15 years* (Resource for Educators, Volume 2) (Council of Europe, 2018a, 2018b). Proficiency assessment was based on the children's oral narratives.

Measures of macrostructure and scoring

Measures of microstructure are relatively easy for teachers to use and understand, which is one of the reasons for their choice over other types of measurements. They can also provide very useful feedback about the stage of narrative development a child has reached, which can help teachers monitor students' progress and intervene with targeted pedagogical practices if necessary.

The study used simple measures of macrostructure because part of the goal was to show teachers how to use narratives in their work without the help of a researcher. Measures such as those used in the Multilingual Assessment Instrument for Narratives (MAIN) (Gagarina *et al.*, 2012), for instance, would have been too complex for non-linguists and less suitable for formative assessment purposes. The task needed to be easy to replicate, so a relatively simple and straightforward evaluation sheet with questions based on the Stein and Glenn (1975) story grammar conceptual framework was selected for use. The sheet is available in Hutson-Nechkash's (1990) guide to structuring oral narratives.

Hutson-Nechkash (1990) developed her evaluation sheet using the descriptions summarised in Table 7.4. These descriptions outline Stein and Glenn's (1975) taxonomy of language development, which is divided into seven different levels. Hutson-Nechkash explains that story grammar assessment is only suitable when children have developed the ability to produce *focused chains* or *true narratives* (Westby, 1984), the difference being the presence or absence of goal-directed behaviour in the narration.

Focused chains include the main character(s) and a logical sequence of events, but a clear goal is still lacking. The approximate time of development is estimated to be around 5 years of age, so just before a child begins the primary school cycle. *True narratives* include the main character(s), a logical sequence of events and a clear goal, while the estimated time of development is 6–7 years of age. Children beginning the primary school cycle are then normally expected to be able to produce true narratives or be close to being able to produce them. Hutson-Nechkash (1990) then goes on to estimate the age of emergence for each level, from birth to 12 years of age, and *true narratives* are meant to correspond to *abbreviated episodes* (see Table 7.5).

Table 7.4 Levels of story grammar development

Level	Sequence type	Description
Level 1	Descriptive Sequence	This story is composed of descriptions of characters, surroundings and usual actions of the characters. No causal relationships of sequences of events are present.
Level 2	Action Sequence	This story consists of events in a chronological order, but no causal relationships exist.
Level 3	Reactive Sequence	This story contains a causal relationship in that certain changes automatically cause other changes. There is no evidence of goal-directed behaviour.
Level 4	Abbreviated Episodes	At this level, a goal is implied, even though it may not be stated explicitly. This story contains either an event statement with a consequence or an internal response with a consequence. The actions of the characters seem to be purposeful though not as well thought out as in successive stages.
Level 5	Complete Episode	This story contains an entire goal-oriented behaviour sequence. A consequence is required as well as two of the following three components: Initiating Event, Internal Response and Attempt.
Level 6	Complex Episode	This level is an elaboration of the complete episode, with an additional partial or complete incident embedded in the episode. A story at this level could also contain multiple plans which are used to achieve the goal. Either one of these factors or both must be present.
Level 7	Interactive Episode	The interactive episode is the highest level. This story contains two characters with separate goals and actions that influence the actions of the other.

Source: Hutson-Nechkash (1990: 18).

Table 7.5 Levels of story grammar development and age of emergence

Age of emergence	Score (%)	Level	Sequence Episode
12/12	100	Level 7	Interactive Episode
11/12	92	Level 6	Complex Episode
10/12	83	Level 6	Complex Episode
9/12	75	Level 5	Complex Episode
8/12	67	Level 5	Complex Episode
7/12	58	Level 4	Abbreviated Episode
6/12	50	Level 4	Abbreviated Episode
5/12	42	Level 3	Reactive Sequence
4/12	33	Level 3	Reactive Sequence
3/12	25	Level 2	Action Sequence
2/12	17	Level 1	Descriptive Sequence
1/12	8	Pre-Level 1	
0/12	0	Pre-Level 1	

Source: Hutson-Nechkash (1990: 15).

Table 7.6 Original evaluation sheet

STORY GRAMMAR ASSESSMENT

NAME:
DATE:

Degrees of structure provided
- No additional structure
- Medium amount of structure
- High degree of structure

1	Is a setting given?	Yes	No
2	Are there characters described?	Yes	No
3	Are the events presented sequentially?	Yes	No
4	Is there a causal relationship between events?	Yes	No
5	Is there an initiating event (IE)?	Yes	No
6	Is a goal present?	Yes	No
7	Is there a consequence?	Yes	No
8	Is an internal response (IR) present?	Yes	No
9	Is there an attempt to attain the goal?	Yes	No
10	Are multiple plans used to meet the goal?	Yes	No
11	Is a partial or complete episode embedded in the episode?	Yes	No
12	Are there two characters with separate goals and actions that influence the action of the other?	Yes	No

Number of YES responses_____/12 × 100 = _____%

Level of story grammar development _____

Source: Hutson-Nechkash (1990: 19).

The original evaluation sheet is reported in Table 7.6. In addition to personal data, the sheet requires information on the degree of structure provided, and then lists 12 'yes/no' questions that need to be answered for the final score to be calculated. The questions are clear, straightforward and easy to use, even for busy teachers.

A total of six evaluation sheets were used, three per story and two for each language.

7.5 Results

Results are organised according to participants' background languages as follows: (1) all multilinguals, (2) Ladin L1 speakers and students with an immigrant background and (3) students with an immigrant background.

The first set of results (all multilinguals) relates to all multilingual students who participated in the study, regardless of whether they were native speakers of Ladin or of another language. Even though their language background varied, the results were first processed for all of them as all students are multilingual and, taken together, they represent the typical student population found in Ladin schools.

The second set of results (Ladin L1 speakers and students with an immigrant background) divides the multilingual group into two main groups: Ladin L1 speakers and all students with an immigrant background. Where relevant, results specific to Ladin schools are provided.

The third set of results (students with an immigrant background) focuses on immigrant students and the association between language proficiency in the languages of narration and narrative abilities in each language.

The data was analysed by a multilingual team of raters with knowledge of the three languages or a reasonable understanding of them. Whenever doubts or concerns arose, extensive consultations between team members took place until a unanimous consensus was reached.

7.5.1 Descriptive summary information

As is the case with most longitudinal research, the study suffered some numerical reduction between the first and the fourth data collection since some children had left the school or were unavailable on the day of the data collection. A summary of participants' information, broken down by school (Ladin, German and Italian in South Tyrol, and Ladin in Fassa/Fascia), language background (Ladin L1 or immigrant background) and languages examined is provided in Table 7.7.

7.5.2 All multilinguals

A summary of the mean scores and standard deviations for each story by language of narration is presented in Table 7.8 and visually presented in Figures 7.2 and 7.3. Analysis of variance (ANOVA) results for both stories are subsequently provided.

Table 7.7 Descriptive participants' information by story, school, language background and language of narration

Story	School	Language background	Language of narration		
			Italian	Ladin	German
The Moon	Ladin, South Tyrol	Immigrant background	8	8	8
		Ladin L1	13	13	13
	Italian, South Tyrol	Immigrant background	7		
	German, South Tyrol	Immigrant background			7
	Ladin, Fassa/Fascia	Immigrant background	7	7	
The Present	Ladin, South Tyrol	Immigrant background	8	7	8
		Ladin L1	13	13	13
	Italian, South Tyrol	Immigrant background	7		
	German, South Tyrol	Immigrant background			7
	Ladin, Fassa/Fascia	Immigrant background	7	7	

Table 7.8 Mean story grammar scores by language of narration and story type

Story	Language	Mean	n	SD
The Moon	Italian	62.37	35	15.98
	German	58.33	24	18.87
	Ladin	66.67	28	18.42
The Present	Italian	58.81	35	14.71
	German	56.25	28	19.85
	Ladin	60.50	27	16.11

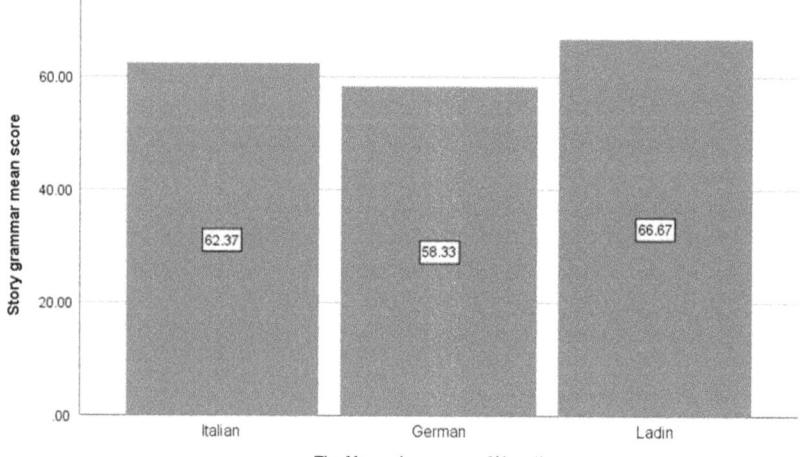

Figure 7.2 *The Moon*: Mean story grammar scores by language of narration

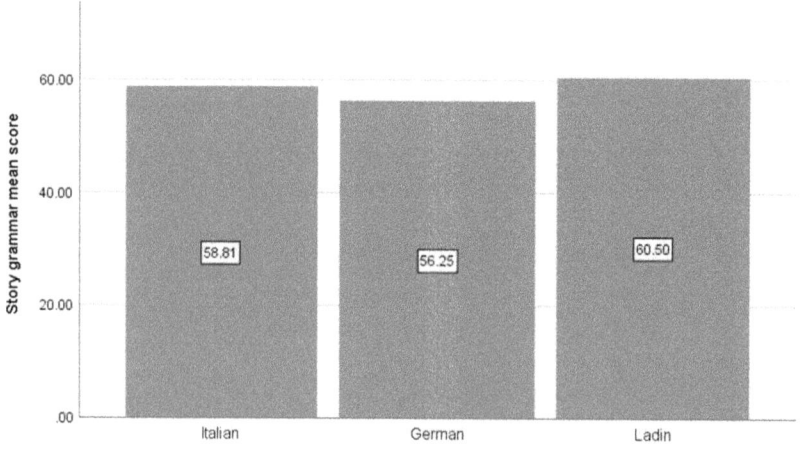

Figure 7.3 *The Present*: Mean story grammar scores by language of narration

An ANOVA with language (Ladin, German and Italian) as the independent variable and story grammar scores as the dependent variable was performed for the narratives produced in the three languages. The analysis was performed for each story independently, and very similar results were obtained. In *The Moon* story, a non-significant difference was found between the language of narration (Italian, German and Ladin) and the story grammar scores at the $p < 0.05$ level $[F(2,84) = 1.45, p = 0.239]$. Likewise, in *The Present* story, a non-significant difference was found between the language of narration (Italian, German and Ladin) and the story grammar scores at the $p < 0.05$ level $[F(2,87) = 0.444, p = 0.643]$. These non-significant results, which are visually represented in Figures 7.2 and 7.3, confirm that the story grammar scores were remarkably stable across the three languages and suggest that participants had similar underlying narrative abilities, regardless of the language of production.

7.5.3 Ladin L1 speakers and students with an immigrant background

Table 7.9 (*The Moon* story) and Table 7.10 (*The Present* story) provide a summary of the mean scores and standard deviations by language

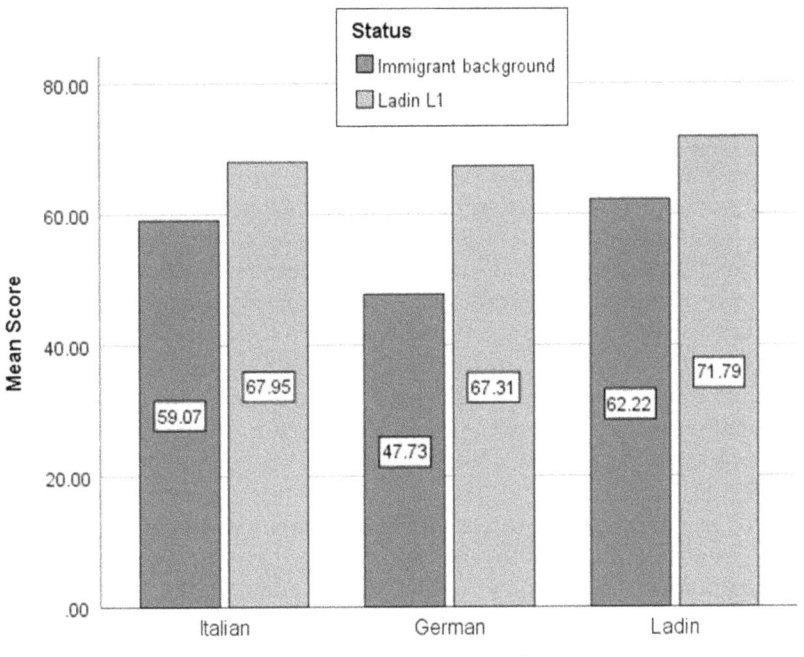

Figure 7.4 Mean scores: *The Moon*

Table 7.9 *The Moon*: Mean story grammar scores by language of narration and students' language background

Language background	Language	Mean	n	SD
Immigrant background	Italian	59.07	22	18.55
	German	47.73	11	20.44
	Ladin	62.22	15	21.56
Ladin L1	Italian	67.95	13	8.23
	German	67.31	13	12.01
	Ladin	71.79	13	12.97

Table 7.10 *The Present*: Mean story grammar scores by language of narration and students' language background

Language background	Language	Mean	n	SD
Immigrant background	Italian	54.92	22	14.92
	German	56.11	15	20.76
	Ladin	57.15	14	15.62
Ladin L1	Italian	65.38	13	12.20
	German	56.41	13	19.59
	Ladin	64.10	13	16.45

and students' language background. The information is also visually presented in Figures 7.4 and 7.5. This is followed by an analysis of macrostructure for the three languages of narration by means of a Kruskal–Wallis test, this time divided by language background (Ladin L1 speakers and students with an immigrant background).

Figures 7.4 and 7.5 visually indicate that Ladin L1 students tend to show higher scores than immigrant students, with the exception of German in *The Present* story. However, the objective was not to compare these two groups to one another, but to examine internal macrostructure stability within each group. An independent Kruskal–Wallis test was therefore conducted to compare the story grammar mean scores for each group (Ladin L1 speakers and students with an immigrant background). No significant differences were identified, which suggests macrostructure stability across languages was retained. The results are summarised in Table 7.11.

So far, the results show macrostructure stability across languages for all multilinguals and then for the two individual groups (Ladin L1 speakers and students with an immigrant background). Tables 7.13 and 7.14 provide a breakdown of the individual story grammar scores obtained by Ladin L1 children and students with an immigrant background for both stories and by language, which gives additional insights into the level of macrostructure stability within each group. In Table 7.12, which

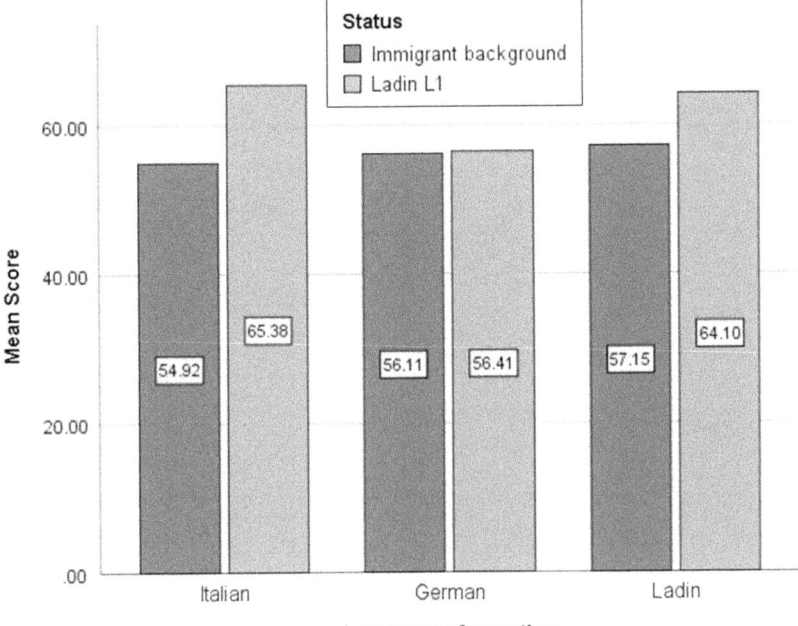

Figure 7.5 Mean scores: *The Present*

Table 7.11 Kruskal–Wallis test results

The Moon	Immigrant background	Kruskal–Wallis	3.507
		Df	2
		Asymp. sig.	0.173
	Ladin L1	Kruskal–Wallis	1.490
		Df	2
		Asymp. sig.	0.475
The Present	Immigrant background	Kruskal–Wallis	0.549
		Df	2
		Asymp. sig.	0.760
	Ladin L1	Kruskal–Wallis	1.265
		Df	2
		Asymp. sig.	0.531

presents results from *The Moon* story, participants with an immigrant background display the highest level of macrostructure instability. Participant 1, for instance, shows a score of 58.33 (Italian), 8.33 (German) and 8.33 (Ladin), while Participant 2 shows stability between Italian and Ladin with a score of 66.67, but 16.66 in German. Ladin L1 participants, on the other hand, show remarkable stability, with scores that are

Table 7.12 *The Moon*: Story grammar scores by school, language background and language of narration

School	Language background	Participant	Age	AoA	Italian	German	Ladin
Ladin	Immigrant background	1	9	0	58.33	8.33	8.33
		2	9	1	66.67	16.66	66.67
		3	12	10	41.66	41.66	–
		4	10	0	41.66	25.00	33.33
		5	11	0	75.00	75.00	75.00
		6	13	6	66.67	66.67	66.67
		7	14	10	66.67	66.67	83.33
		8	13	0	–	58.33	50.00
		9	16	13	33.33	33.33	66.67
	Ladin L1	10	9	0	66.66	25.00	66.66
		11	8	0	50.00	50.00	58.33
		12	9	0	75.00	66.66	50.00
		13	9	0	58.33	58.33	50.00
		14	9	0	66.66	50.00	75.00
		15	10	0	58.33	66.66	75.00
		15	10	0	75.00	83.33	91.97
		17	11	0	66.66	58.33	66.66
		18	12	0	75.00	83.33	83.33
		19	12	0	75.00	75.00	83.33
		20	13	0	75.00	75.00	75.00
		21	13	0	66.67	66.67	75.00
		22	14	0	75.00	83.33	83.33
Fassa	Immigrant background	23	8	2	41.67	–	41.67
		24	10	4	75.00	–	75.00
		25	10	3	75.00	–	83.33
		26	11	6	83.33	–	83.33
		27	14	5	83.33	–	83.33
		28	13	4	58.33	–	58.33
		29	13	3	–	–	83.33

mostly within ±1 of the levels of story grammar development outlined in Table 7.5, and show evidence of the ability to produce complex episodes. According to Table 7.5, at 5 years of age a normally developing child is expected to reach a score of 42% (Level 3, Reactive Sequence) and at 6 years of age a score of 50% (Level 4, Abbreviated Episode). Since all the participants in the study were healthy, typically developing children, they should all have obtained a minimum score of 50%. This is, however, not the case for narrative production scores in several languages, which

Table 7.13 *The Present*: Story grammar scores by school, language background and language of narration

School	Language background	Participant	Age	AoA	Italian	German	Ladin
Ladin	Immigrant background	1	9	0	41.66	16.67	–
		2	9	1	58.33	33.33	66.67
		3	12	10	41.66	66.67	–
		4	10	0	41.66	58.33	33.33
		5	11	0	75.00	50.00	83.33
		6	13	6	41.66	50.00	41.66
		7	14	10	41.66	50.00	41.66
		8	13	0	–	75.00	41.66
		9	16	13	41.66	50.00	50.00
	Ladin L1	10	9	0	41.66	25.00	50.00
		11	8	0	41.66	50.00	58.33
		12	9	0	75.00	91.67	75.00
		13	9	0	66.67	33.33	66.67
		14	9	0	75.00	41.66	66.67
		15	10	0	66.67	58.33	41.67
		15	10	0	66.67	83.33	83.33
		17	11	0	58.33	91.67	50.00
		18	12	0	58.33	50.00	50.00
		19	12	0	–	58.33	83.33
		20	13	0	–	58.33	41.67
		21	13	0	–	75.00	83.33
		22	14	0	–	91.67	83.33
Fassa	Immigrant background	23	8	2	41.67	–	41.67
		24	10	4	66.67	–	75.00
		25	10	3	75.00	–	83.33
		26	11	6	83.33	–	83.33
		27	14	5	83.33	–	83.33
		28	13	4	58.33	–	58.33
		29	13	3	58.33	–	83.33

suggests macrostructure stability is strongly connected to language proficiency. None of the Ladin L1 children fell below the 50% threshold in all languages, while several students with an immigrant background did so, as the results in Tables 7.12 and 7.13 show.

Further confirmation that macrostructure stability is connected to language proficiency comes from the analysis of mean scores and language proficiency. These results, which are summarised in Table 7.14, show that none of the participants with a score below the 50% threshold

Table 7.14 *The Moon* and *The Present*: CEFR and mean scores by language

Language of narration	CEFR	Mean	n	SD
Italian	A1	41.67	2	0.00
	A1+	31.24	4	7.97
	A2	58.99	25	16.49
	A2+	61.11	9	12.50
	B1	68.75	4	7.97
German	Pre-A1	35.42	4	23.94
	A1	35.41	4	4.17
	A1+	44.45	3	4.81
	A2	51.39	6	15.29
	A2+	70.83	6	15.59
	B1	66.66	2	23.57
	B1+	83.33	1	–
Ladin	Pre-A1	8.33	1	–
	A1	54.17	8	13.36
	A2	61.81	12	18.62
	A2+	68.75	8	13.18

had reached the CEFR A2 level. While numbers in each category were too low for further analysis, there is a noticeable trend of scores increasing as proficiency level increases.

7.5.4 Frequency of language use

Parents were asked to estimate how often their children used their languages during a typical day outside of the school context, and this information was combined with the known exposure to the three languages of instruction at school. The estimated frequency of language use was then examined for each group, the results of which are visually presented in Figure 7.6. Even though participant numbers are relatively low, meaning the information would need to be verified with a larger subject pool, the data suggests that, between the exposure at school and outside of the school contexts, Ladin L1 children use the three languages of instruction in a fairly balanced manner. Italian and German are the languages most used (33.82% and 34.13%, respectively) followed by Ladin, which is used 29.13% of the time. The last category (Other) is minimal (2.92%). Students with an immigrant background instead show a rather different pattern. Starting from the Other category, these children speak a language that is different from the three languages of instruction 26.39% of the time. German is used 24.29% of the time, Italian 41.55% and Ladin 7.77% of the time. Ladin is the least-used language by children with an immigrant background.

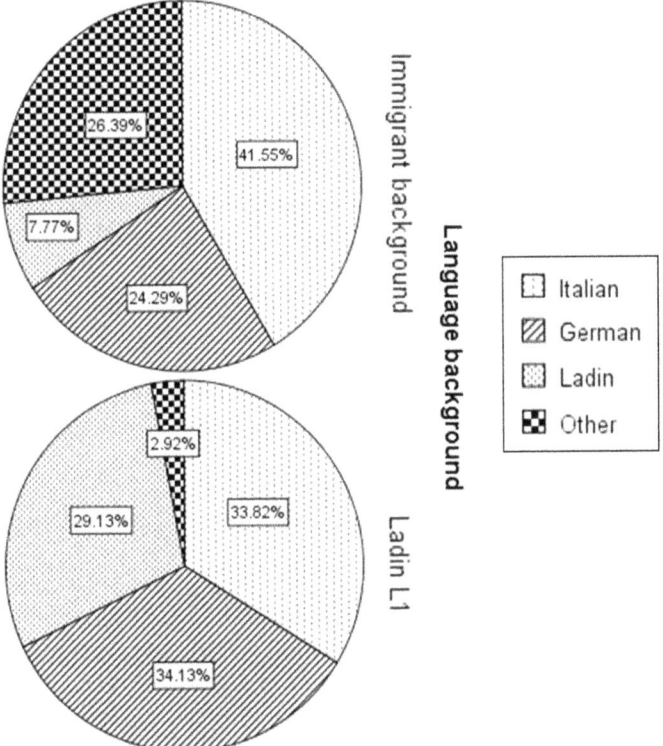

Figure 7.6 Italian, German and Ladin: estimate of daily language use at home and school

7.6 Discussion

The Ladin school board runs a trilingual (Ladin, German, Italian) education system attended by students with very different language backgrounds. Principals and teachers working in a system of this kind often wonder to what extent an immigrant child can learn three languages simultaneously and also learn content through these languages from an early age. Furthermore, many wonder whether it would not be wiser to introduce the languages of instruction more gradually, perhaps one at a time, so as to give the student more time to focus on one or two languages before they concentrate on the third one. Answering such complex questions requires detailed and up-to-date information, and it is understandable that schools turn to multilingualism research for guidance and support. However, giving advice on these matters is not as straightforward as one may think, because language development is deeply affected by a number of factors, such as the student's language background and the quality and quantity of input students receive, i.e. the languages they already know and those spoken within the school and the living environment. A discussion about testing and assessment, multilingualism and language development should therefore engage with these two factors, which are at the heart of the integrated approach to testing and assessment proposed in this volume.

This discussion section first provides an overview of how the integrated approach to testing and assessment was used to design the test for the South Tyrol study, including a summary of its main features and the reasons behind many of the choices made. The section then moves on to discuss the study's research questions in more detail.

7.6.1 The integrated approach and the South Tyrol study

The study's conceptualisation was guided by the integrated approach to testing and assessment, which informed each of the decisions made during the test design process. The study provides an example of the flexibility that the integrated approach offers and shows how test writers can design a test and select the options that are best suited for the test takers' profiles.

The participants in the study have very diverse language profiles. Some of the students are Ladin L1 speakers born and raised in South Tyrol and have therefore regularly been exposed to the three languages of instruction since birth through the family environment and/or the community; other students are first- or second-generation immigrants used to speaking languages other than the languages of instruction in the family context. The study examined differences in performance between these two groups, focusing on the development of narrative abilities in the three languages.

Narratives were chosen for several reasons. First, narratives are regularly taught in school using different languages, so all participants would have been very comfortable with completing activities that involved the use of several languages. Second, narratives are part of every child's life, as most parents tend to read or tell stories to their children long before they start school, so most children would have started to develop their narrative ability from a very young age. Third, narratives, especially story grammars, are particularly suited to examining the relationship between language proficiency and narrative development. While narratives were deemed ideal for the purpose of our study, it is also relevant to note that tests can be designed using different goals, contents and materials. The test presented in this chapter is only meant to be one example of how the integrated approach can be used in education, not an example of the best type of test to be used in education.

Returning to our study, since students had different proficiency levels in the languages of instruction, it was a priority to elicit narrative production in each individual language so that the relationship between the level of proficiency achieved in each language and the stage of macrostructure stability between languages could be assessed. The use of a monolingual task does not, however, mean that the test was entirely monolingual, as a traditional monolingual approach would envisage. The test was, in fact, a *multilingual-by-design* test, as some flexibility was applied during scoring by accepting the occasional use of words in a language other than the language of narration.

A test design must be suitable for the purpose of testing, which in this case was formative in nature, and for the questions being asked. The test was intended to provide useful feedback about the progress being made by students with an immigrant background while they are exposed to multiple languages at school. Had the students been given the opportunity to narrate the story by mixing languages at will – as a translanguaging approach would postulate – it would not have been possible to answer any of the questions asked and therefore identify potential threshold levels for narrative abilities in individual languages.

The materials used in the study were deliberately simple and straightforward to use as one of the objectives was to enable teachers to assess narrative abilities independently after the study had been completed. While teachers will never be required to carry out the type of detailed analysis presented above, they can easily use a form containing 12 questions and calculate a simple percentage that can provide them with valuable information about the students' stage of narrative development at any point during the school year.

As far as the input modality is concerned, the test was made more suitable for a culturally and linguistically diverse student population by introducing a silent video, so that students with poor language skills would not be disadvantaged by comprehension difficulties. Moreover, since the task had to be completed in several individual languages, it was essential to show a video that did not provide any kind of language input. The test was then administered by school staff who were familiar with all the languages of instruction and could answer questions in any language. A summary of how the integrated approach to testing and assessment was applied in the study is provided in Table 7.15. A more detailed description of the individual categories listed in the table can be found in Chapter 5.

7.6.2 Macrostructure stability

The first research question was: Do multilingual children's narratives vary between three languages with regard to macrostructure?

Given the amount of evidence of macrostructure stability in bilingual narratives (Altman *et al.*, 2016; Hipfner-Boucher *et al.*, 2014; Iluz-Cohen & Walters, 2012; Pearson, 2002; Uccelli & Páez, 2007), there is, in principle, no reason why the same stability should not be confirmed in multilingual narratives. The number of languages known, however, is not the only variable that needs to be considered. An equally crucial factor is

Table 7.15 The integrated approach to testing and assessment as applied to the South Tyrol study

Purpose Test construct	Formative Story grammar, narrative macrostructure
Population	Multilinguals: (a) Ladin L1 speakers with knowledge of German and Italian (b) First- and second-generation immigrants with variable L1s, exposed to the three languages of instruction at school and within the community context
Test format	Multilingual-by-design: Monolingual narrative task combined with multilingual scoring
Test input: Instructions	Oral – in the language of testing
Test input: Content	No language – silent video
Test output	Oral – in the language of testing
Scoring	Flexible – words in a language other than the language of narration accepted
Interpretation	Two levels: (a) All multilinguals (b) Ladin L1 speakers and all students with an immigrant background

proficiency in the background languages, since some elements of macrostructure may emerge only when a proficiency threshold has been reached.

The production of coherent narrative structures with goal–attempt–outcome sequences requires a level of proficiency that recently immigrated children may not have had the time to develop. It may take some time before newly arrived immigrants are able to use even a simple internal structure and proficiency thresholds are currently unknown. To my knowledge, there are no published studies on narratives in three or more languages, so this is the first study that provides information on macrostructure stability between languages and the extent to which language proficiency plays a role in the stabilisation process.

Overall, results seem to confirm macrostructure stability across languages. When all multilingual students are examined together as a single group, mean score differences between languages are non-significant for both *The Moon* story (Italian, 62.37; German, 58.33; Ladin, 66.67) and *The Present* story (Italian, 58.81; German, 56.25; Ladin, 60.50). When Ladin L1 students and students with an immigrant background are examined as separate groups, however, a slightly different picture emerges. While no differences are found in relation to macrostructure stability within each group, some differences between groups were identified, with Ladin L1 students generally showing more advanced narrative abilities than students with an immigrant background. An exception to this was the German production of *The Present* story, which appeared balanced across groups. These differences, visually shown in Figures 7.4 and 7.5, were not analysed further, because the objective was not to compare individuals with different profiles with one another but to evaluate macrostructure stability within each individual group.

Some of the immigrant students were of recent immigration, so the likelihood that these students lowered the overall average for the group is high. Since these students were only few in number (see Tables 7.13 and 7.14), it was not possible to further divide them into groups according to age of arrival. However, the majority of these students were born and raised in South Tyrol or had reached South Tyrol prior to the age of 5, i.e. before starting primary school, so, given their long period of residence in the area, it can be assumed that they had had a fair amount of exposure to the languages of instruction or at least to Italian and/or German, which are widely spoken in the region.

From a language acquisition perspective, we know that quality and quantity of input play a crucial role in the learning process (Cook, 2016; Gass & Selinker, 2008; Mitchell *et al.*, 2013; Myles, 2010; Saville-Troike & Barto, 2017). One of the key differences between Ladin L1 speakers and students with an immigrant background is related to the frequency of use of the languages of instruction in daily life, i.e. at school and within the family and community contexts. While Ladin L1 students show a balanced exposure to the three languages (Italian 33.82%, German 34.13% and Ladin 29.13%), students with an immigrant background do not. Exposure to Italian is quite consistent (41.55%), followed by German (24.29%) and Ladin (7.77%), but a considerable amount of time is also devoted to using other languages (26.39%), most typically the home languages. Frequency of use may also explain why immigrant children from the Fassa/Fascia Valley seem to show above average story grammar scores, even though none of these students was born in Italy. In the Fassa/Fascia Valley, the most common languages are two very similar Romance languages: Ladin and Italian. Children in the Fassa/Fascia Valley thus learn to communicate in fewer languages than those in South Tyrol as German is not as widespread, so students probably benefited from the extra time spent using two languages, as opposed to three, that are also mutually intelligible and typologically similar to one another.

The data on frequency of use further confirms the importance of taking into account individual language profiles and languages spoken within the community when interpreting test scores, as test results can be read differently, depending on the students' language background and the languages spoken within their community. Further research should focus on the role of these two factors in students' test performance, and the overall implications for large-scale assessment should be evaluated more closely.

7.6.3 Background languages and language proficiency

The second and third research questions were: (2) Do multilingual children perform differently at different proficiency levels? and (3) Can a threshold level be identified for cross-linguistic influence to arise in relation to macrostructure?

Results seem to confirm macrostructure stability between languages within each group, but differences between groups suggest that narrative abilities are sensitive to differences in proficiency levels. Very little is currently known about the way language proficiency influences the development of narrative abilities across multiple languages as most studies have focused on bilingual narratives, and one of the languages was always the native language. An answer to the question of whether children behave differently at different levels of competence implies that we are able to identify a point of emergence for cross-linguistic influence in production. In other words, if a child develops the ability to narrate in his/her native language up to any given point along the narrative scale (see Tables 7.4 and 7.5), when (i.e. at what proficiency level) is the child able to transfer this knowledge to another language? Unfortunately, we were not in a position to ask the children to tell the story in their native language, but, since all the children were typically developing children, we can safely assume that all of them had reached the 50% threshold of a normally developing child at 6 years of age.

Individual scores mostly reflect macrostructure stability when scores are above 50% or, in a few cases, above 41.66%. Narrative macrostructure instead appears to be highly unstable whenever story grammar scores are below 41.66%. In order to obtain a score of 41.66%, the narrative had to have included the setting, a description of the characters, a sequence of events, cause–effect relationships and an initiating event. What would be typically missing is goal-directed behaviour, which allows characters to set a plan and carry out one or more attempts to solve the problem described in the initiating event. It is reasonable to assume that at least a CEFR A2 level would be required to go beyond the initial descriptive details (setting, characters, initial event) so the threshold level can be provisionally placed around the CEFR A2 proficiency level for language and between 41.66% and 50% for narrative abilities. No child with an average score below 44.45% had a proficiency level above the CEFR A1+ level, which suggests that an individual may acquire narrative abilities in any language and use those abilities across multiple languages, as long as a minimal threshold of language proficiency has been reached. The data also shows a possible association between story grammar scores and CEFR levels for each language, with a clear rising trend between grammar scores and CEFR levels. While numbers were too low to conduct further analysis, with the data available it seems reasonable to set the threshold level to A2 and claim a positive association between story grammar mean scores and CEFR levels. Further research would be required to confirm these conclusions with a larger subject pool.

The ability to narrate a story develops over time and one other possibility worth considering in future research is that differences in proficiency levels may be linked to the speed of narrative development, with some elements appearing at different stages of development. For example, telling a story that includes a setting and one or more characters does not require advanced language proficiency and early descriptive elements may appear relatively quickly (basic narrative skills), while adding sequences that include goal-directed behaviour and multiple plots is a more complex task that requires more advanced language knowledge and therefore more time to reach the required level (advanced narrative skills). Progression from basic to advanced narrative skills may thus depend on the proficiency level in the language of narration.

7.6.4 Second language proficiency and potential threshold levels

Discussions about the way L2 proficiency affects students' performance typically centre around the unfairness of expecting students to achieve native-like standards of performance that we already know non-native speakers cannot achieve in a non-dominant language. The South Tyrol study provides further confirmation that many immigrant students cannot be expected to perform like the majority of the student population in Ladin schools and that a minimum level of language proficiency is required for them to perform effectively.

The purpose of our test was formative in nature, whose aim was to examine the South Tyrol reality and gather useful evidence that could support teachers in their work. Overall results suggest that immigrant children who have not reached the A2 level in the language of narration are not likely to be able to engage in a narrative task in a meaningful way. Results also show that the ability to tell a story is independent of the language of narration. A child may be able to tell a story and introduce advanced goal-directed behaviour features in one language but not in others, but once the threshold level has been reached, narrative abilities seem to transfer easily across languages. This information can be very useful for teachers, who need to plan teaching activities for a class while taking into account that some students may not be able to follow the lesson due to poor language skills. With a greater awareness of threshold levels, teachers can initially aim to increase the child's level of competence up to the CEFR A2 level in the language(s) of narration and subsequently focus on developing the child's narrative skills with targeted activities appropriate to the level of competence achieved.

Information on threshold levels is also essential for schools that wish to advise families on language practices at home. Immigrant parents often turn to schools and teachers for advice about the extent to which the native language should be used in the home environment. Parents want their children to be successful, and knowledge of the language of instruction is typically considered an essential component of success. Parents of children entering a trilingual education system are often anxious, as the child needs to learn several languages to complete the school cycle successfully. When immigrant parents approach schools with their doubts and concerns, it is not uncommon for well-meaning principals or teachers to advise them to help the child focus on the languages of instruction, leading to an inevitable decrease in the time spent using the L1 in the home. Instead, schools can play a crucial role in the child's cognitive development by helping families understand that reading stories in the child's native language helps the child develop narrative abilities that will eventually transfer to the languages of instruction, whenever the child is linguistically ready for transfer to occur.

If children do not develop narrative abilities through the L1, they will have no abilities to transfer to any language when they reach the required threshold level in the languages of instruction. Teachers may erroneously assume the child has a language proficiency issue when the problem may be that the child has not developed narrative abilities in any language so he/she cannot perform effectively. Teachers should also make sure that language knowledge is separated from narrative abilities, as this will help them avoid falling into the trap of thinking that students need to learn more language when what they need is the time to develop their narrative abilities. Parents should also be made aware that listening to stories in the home language is an essential part of the learning process and will teach the child crucial abilities that will eventually transfer to the languages of instruction when the child reaches the required level.

8 Looking Ahead

The field of multilingual testing and assessment has seen slow theoretical progress over the years, mainly because the work produced has been largely based on bilingual rather than multilingual data, with the inevitable limitations that this entails. Bilinguals and multilinguals are very different populations with very different requirements, particularly when they live in multilingual contexts and/or attend multilingual educational programmes, and the almost exclusive focus on bilinguals and second language (L2) speakers has created a significant void in the field that has reduced our overall ability to understand how to manage multilingual students in testing and how to approach the task of designing tests that are suitable for a broad range of culturally and linguistically diverse student populations.

This volume has extended existing discussions to include multilinguals with very different language profiles, ranging from immigrant students with poor language skills to minority language speakers with good knowledge of the languages of instruction. It has also proposed using an integrated approach to testing and assessment with the aim of providing a flexible solution that can overcome the barriers posed by traditional and holistic approaches to testing and assessment. Central to this approach is the difference between (1) designing multilingual tests and (2) assessing multilingual individuals. The approach proposes to focus on how tests are designed, administered, scored and interpreted and suggests a way of managing individual variability and different sociolinguistic contexts by combining the individual and the social dimensions, i.e. multilinguals' language background (individual) and the languages spoken in the communities in which they live (social).

This chapter begins with some considerations about designing multilingual tests (Section 8.1) before moving on to review why the way multilinguals are currently classified in testing needs to be changed (Section 8.2). This is followed by a discussion of the role of testing in shaping multilinguals' perceptions of their own language skills (Section 8.3) and some further reflections on the nature of multilingual communication

(Section 8.4). The chapter ends with some concluding remarks on ways of moving forward.

8.1 Designing Multilingual Tests

Assessing multilingual students requires the use of tests that are suitable for culturally and linguistically diverse student populations, but not everyone agrees on what makes a test suitable for such a population.

For decades, the testing industry, teachers and educators have been used to thinking that a test can only be monolingual, i.e. it can only be written in one language and cannot contain instructions or content in different languages. Some form of cultural and linguistic simplifications can be applied, but for most test writers, a test remains essentially monolingual. Holistic approaches to testing and assessment propose to overcome this conceptual barrier by including examinees' languages in the test design, so that both comprehension and production are facilitated and students are not placed at a significant disadvantage in comparison to their monolingual peers. This is a viable solution in many homogeneous bilingual, or at most trilingual, contexts, whereas it is not viable when several languages are to be included in the test.

The integrated approach to testing and assessment proposes an intermediate solution that conceives the stages of test design, administration, scoring and interpretation as individual blocks or units, so that test writers can choose the most suitable language option for each unit, and all decisions, such as how the test is administered, scored and interpreted, can be taken accordingly. This gives a level of flexibility that allows test writers to combine monolingual and multilingual elements in the test, as explained in Chapter 5. Flexibility is of paramount importance in this process because multilingual tests are much more complex to design than bilingual tests, and the underlying rationale of the test writing process is that the approach must be flexible enough to adapt to different types of test takers and sociolinguistic contexts.

The integrated approach to testing and assessment shifts the focus from the way multilinguals use their languages in communication, i.e. fluidly and freely switching between languages, to who the test takers are and where they live, combining the individual and the social dimensions. This shifts the attention from trying to find ways to be fair to multilingual students by focusing on the languages they use in daily communication, to trying to be fair to them by classifying them for who they are. Emphasis is also placed on the living environment, as the sociolinguistic environment is well known to influence the speed and rate of language acquisition in language learners. Since a test does not end with a test score, the test interpretation stage is also given more of a central role, as it is at this stage that students' scores can be analysed and their performance compared with that of students with similar language profiles who live in similar sociolinguistic contexts.

8.2 Classifying Multilinguals in Testing

The way in which bilinguals and multilinguals are classified in testing represents a considerable challenge for the testing industry, because the use of an incorrect classification can introduce a significant bias in the testing process. The way test takers are classified in testing is closely linked to the wider problem of having to distinguish between examinees who are native speakers of the language of testing and those for whom the language of testing is a non-dominant language. The distinction is necessary because a test that gives one group of examinees an advantage over another can be considered a biased test, and in multilingual testing those who speak the language of testing as a non-dominant language are at a considerable disadvantage compared to those for whom the language of testing is the native language.

The testing industry has been actively working towards finding a solution to the language proficiency problem. Up to now, the preferred solution has been to modify monolingual tests in order to make them more suitable for linguistically and culturally diverse student populations. This type of intervention entails introducing changes that modify the test itself, without needing any type of engagement with the test takers. An example of this type of intervention is cultural and linguistic simplification, which is assumed to make the test easier to understand for those who have low proficiency in the language of testing.

Another solution that is only partially adopted by the testing industry relates to focusing on the test takers and their language profiles, i.e. group membership. Standardised tests routinely classify students using a very limited number of categories, such as first language (L1)/native speaker, first-generation immigrant and second-generation immigrant. These categories address the language proficiency problem only in part because they fail to capture all those bilinguals and multilinguals who are minority language speakers who have never moved from their native land (see Section 2.3.3). Ladin students in South Tyrol are an example of this, as in standardised tests they are typically tested in Italian, which is not their mother tongue, but they cannot be classified as immigrants in any way. Students who live in similar bilingual and multilingual communities are scattered around the world.

The integrated approach to testing and assessment places major emphasis on students' language profiles precisely because many multilingual students are frequently classified incorrectly in testing. To address the language proficiency problem, an alternative approach would be to classify test takers according to their language background (group membership) and use the classification to interpret test scores, thus ensuring that only students with similar profiles are compared to one other, i.e. L1 speakers are compared to L1 speakers, first-generation immigrants to first-generation immigrants and so forth.

As a linguist, whenever I come across the questionnaires commonly used to classify test takers for assessment purposes, I am particularly concerned about the lack of information they require about students' prior language background and living environment. While the goal of standardised tests is to assess the overall quality of educational systems – whether national or international – the 'system' is evaluated by testing individuals, and the more inaccurate the classification of the student population, the less reliable and the more biased the results will be.

The negative impact of misclassification can be intuitively perceived, but the problem has not been systematically discussed in the international literature, particularly with regard to multilingual students. There are, in my view, manageable forms of improvement that can be considered. One obvious way to achieve more realistic classifications would be to add new categories to the existing ones that reflect students' actual profiles, such as *functional bilingual* or *functional multilingual*, and to gather information about the examinees' living environment. The additional information would ensure minority language speakers would not be classified as native speakers of the language of testing but as *functional bilinguals* or *functional multilinguals* who live in multilingual sociolinguistic settings. One difficulty associated with this solution is that the categories used to classify test takers must be mutually exclusive. This may well give rise to ambiguities which can, however, be easily resolved using the information available about students' language backgrounds and their living environment, assuming it is collected. The advantage of being able to provide a better way of classifying multilingual speakers outweighs the possible challenges associated with defining new categories and revising existing ones in order not to create categories that overlap.

The introduction of more accurate ways of classifying test takers implies an acceptance that students' language background and living environment may have a significant impact on test scores and therefore constitute a significant bias in testing. The creation of new categories is no doubt complex to implement, but it is worth the effort because standardised testing remains central to the evaluation of multilingual education programmes around the world, and most of these programmes were originally established to cater for local minority language populations (see Chapter 3). Moreover, results must be sufficiently accurate and reliable to avoid discriminating in favour of one group of examinees over another, as standardised tests are regularly used to assess the quality of education worldwide and results can affect the lives of millions of people.

As we have seen in the South Tyrol study, most of the students attending Ladin schools are Ladin L1 speakers, and only a small number of students are of immigrant origin. When Ladin L1 speakers take national standardised tests such as the INVALSI test, they cannot be classified correctly due to a lack of suitable categories. These students are typically L2 speakers of the language of testing but cannot be classified as first- or second-generation immigrants because neither they nor their parents have ever left their native land for several generations. They are also students who are exposed to a minimum of three languages at school and in the living environment and who devote about a third of their time to each language (see Figure 7.6). Most Ladin L1 students are then asked to take a standardised test that is not designed for them, yet the effectiveness of the Ladin school system is evaluated on the basis of how these students perform, with the expectation that they will perform like native speakers, as it is native speakers with whom they will eventually be compared.

8.3 Multilinguals' Perceptions of Their Own Language Competence

Having observed the behaviour of linguistic minorities for many years, particularly in South Tyrol, on several occasions I was able to observe how these populations develop a somewhat distorted perception of their own language skills. Although they speak several languages fluently, after years and years of being compared with monolingual speakers and the general expectation from school and society that they reach a level of competence comparable to that of native speakers, it is not surprising that they always feel one step behind. This is a phenomenon of linguistic insecurity that affects many minority populations, which in the modern world has been reinforced by the extensive misuse of testing in education. Recognising the need to assess functional multilinguals for their linguistic uniqueness would help to offset the negative message that these populations have always received, viz. that their own multilingualism is nothing special, when in fact it is a major individual achievement.

When I first went to live in South Tyrol, I was fascinated by the high level of language fluency that people have in the region and the frequent language mixing I heard, especially in public places such as shops, hospitals and public offices. I also noticed a widespread lack of confidence, as most of these multilinguals seemed to feel inadequate and somewhat 'faulty' when it came to their own language skills. I still remember a conversation I had in Italian with a German native speaker from South Tyrol, a young student who communicated with me in impeccable Italian. Had I not known that she was a native German speaker, I would never have noticed that she had a mother tongue other than Italian. However, at a certain point in the conversation, she felt the need to apologise for her Italian, using the excuse that Italian was for her an L2. If, on the one hand, these statements are used as identity markers, on the other I remember being surprised by how unaware she seemed of how good her Italian was. While all scholars with an interest in multilingualism would fully appreciate that in multilingual areas such as South Tyrol the L1 cannot be easily separated from matters of personal identity and ethnicity, I still found that adding the L2 label to such beautiful and in-depth knowledge of a language clashed with my own notion of fluency.

The way minorities perceive their language skills is deeply connected to testing, as it is through school performance that they will have received most of the messages that their language knowledge is somehow defective. Over time, the use of fairer and more equitable forms of testing will empower these populations and help them change the way they perceive their own language abilities. The very need to empower individuals is based on the assumption that something has been lost or weakened, whether a sense of identity, self-esteem or language skills, and that the loss has affected their perception of who they are. The empowerment of multilingual minority language speakers goes far beyond their right to show what they know when taking a test or being tested in a language they fully understand. It means recognising they are unique and different and helping them understand and appreciate why this is the case. A significant step in the right direction would be to start classifying them correctly in testing and to stop comparing them with monolinguals. This will ultimately help them learn to appreciate their own multilingualism as an immense resource rather than an obstacle and to recognise the privilege they have had in growing up exposed to multiple languages in their lives.

8.4 Monolingual and Multilingual Communication

In this volume, we have seen how many researchers are calling for changes in testing that give multilingual students more autonomy and allow them to communicate with the fluidity they are used to. I have been growing increasingly uncomfortable with the idea of conceiving the fluidity of communication as multilinguals' most natural way of communicating, because this view implies that multilingual communication is natural while monolingual communication is not.

Human communication depends on many factors, such as the formality or informality of the conversation, the context of an exchange, the purpose of communication and the languages the interlocutor speaks. If informal communication allows languages to be freely mixed and informal expressions to be used when the interlocutor shares the same languages as the speaker, this does not mean that multilingual individuals can go to a job interview and freely mix their languages with the interviewer, as such behaviour would only result in the speaker not being offered the job. On the other hand, in some professional contexts, the ability to engage in bilingual or multilingual communication may be an asset and it may be wise to display an ability to use two or more languages fluidly in communication.

In professional contexts, the demand that the employee functions in one language is widespread, while the ability to speak individual languages remains a skill sought by many companies. Future employees are often required to provide evidence of language proficiency and usually take language proficiency exams for this purpose. Even if multilingual tests were introduced instead of monolingual ones, employers would still want to know something about future employees' language skills in individual languages. In other words, there will always be a market for monolingual testing, which currently serves millions of bilingual and multilingual individuals working around the world and students trying to get into third-level education abroad. The law of the market is that, as long as there is demand, there will be an offer.

If I consider the book-writing activity in which I'm currently engaging, I can say it is essentially a monolingual activity. This book is being written for professional reasons, and I am using English as the main language of written communication. English is not my native language and, while I may find it convenient to be able to switch between English and my native Italian, the final product would certainly be a messy piece of writing unfit for the purpose of professional communication, even if the book is presumably going to be read by an audience with an interest in multilingualism. My point here is that while multiple language speakers frequently mix their languages in communication – as I do with my family and friends – multilinguals are required to function monolingually on many occasions, which can happen in the social context, the work environment, at school, in hospital or while shopping. While the field of multilingual testing and assessment must find ways to reach those students for whom current assessment practices are unfair and can put them at a disadvantage, we must not lose sight of the fact that language mixing is not considered normal in many situations and that students should also learn to function monolingually. If current monolingual assessment practices convey the message that multilingualism is a problem rather than a resource, replacing monolingual practices with multilingual ones will send the message that monolingual communication is not important in life. Language mixing may even have detrimental effects on learning, as it would be very tempting for students to fill knowledge gaps by using other language sources available to them rather than putting in the effort to improve their proficiency in individual languages.

The integrated approach to testing and assessment attempted to find a middle ground between traditional and holistic approaches to multilingual testing and assessment, with the intention of providing the flexibility needed to meet the many different communicative situations multilinguals are likely to encounter in their lives. Since human communication can naturally occur along any point of the monolingualism–multilingualism continuum, we should be willing to find solutions in testing that can accommodate communication taking place at both extremes and any point in between.

8.5 Concluding Comment

The discussions on multilingual testing and assessment included in this volume have been developed with the full awareness that those working in the testing industry and many of the academics and educators working on multilingualism need to establish a constructive form of dialogue to enable them to truly resolve the many challenges I have outlined.

I started this book by discussing the Black-and-White Fallacy and how current academic discourse is polarised at two incompatible extremes: the use of monolingual tests with multilingual speakers (traditional approach) and the use of multiple languages within individual tests (holistic approach). I proposed the *integrated approach to testing and assessment* as a mediating position aiming to start building a bridge between the two sides. This volume will hopefully make the testing industry sufficiently aware of the need to improve the way multilinguals are classified in testing and that the heterogeneity of the student population can be addressed by recognising the importance of group membership and the languages spoken within the living community. I also hope that those in favour of the idea of using multiple languages in testing will consider each stage of the testing process with an open mind and learn to recognise that monolingualism is a natural form of communication for multilinguals, just like language mixing and code-switching, and that mixed forms of testing are possible and would, in fact, mirror the way multilinguals *naturally* use their languages in communication.

As I have shown in this volume, there is no single way to test multilingual student populations, just as there is no single way to write multilingual tests. There is, however, only one way to move forward, and that is by establishing constructive dialogue between those who hold different positions and expressing a common willingness to explore solutions that are truly workable and suitable for linguistically and culturally diverse student populations and the classroom context.

References

Abedi, J. (2006) Language issues in item development. In S.M. Downing and T.M. Haladyna (eds) *Handbook of Test Development* (pp. 377–398). Mahwah, NJ: Lawrence Erlbaum Associates.

Abedi, J. and Lord, C. (2001) The language factor in mathematics tests. *Applied Measurement in Education* 14 (3), 219–234.

Abedi, J. and Gándara, P. (2006) Performance of English language learners as a subgroup in large-scale assessment: Interaction of research and policy. *Educational Measurement Issues and Practice* 25 (4), 36–46.

Abedi, J., Hofstetter, C., Baker, E. and Lord, C. (2001) NAEP Math Performance and Test Accommodations: Interactions with Student Language Background (CSE Technical Report 536). The National Center for Research on Evaluation, Standards, and Student Testing, Los Angeles, CA.

Abedi, J., Courtney, M., Mirocha, J., Leon, S. and Goldberg, J. (2005) Language Accommodations for English Language Learners in Large-Scale Assessments: Bilingual Dictionaries and Linguistic Modification (CSE Report 666). The National Center for Research on Evaluation, Standards, and Student Testing, Los Angeles, CA.

Adamson, B. and Feng, A. (2014) Models for trilingual education in the People's Republic of China. In D. Gorter, V. Zenotz and J. Cenoz (eds) *Minority Languages and Multilingual Education* (pp. 29–44). Dordrecht: Springer. doi: https://doi.org/10.1007/978-94-007-7317-2_3

Allalouf, A., Hambleton, R.K. and Sireci, S.G. (1999) Identifying the causes of differential item functioning in translated verbal items. *Journal of Educational Measurement* 36 (3), 185–198.

Altman, C., Armon-Lotem, S., Fichman, S. and Walters, J. (2016) Macrostructure, microstructure, and mental state terms in the narratives of English–Hebrew bilingual preschool children with and without specific language impairment. *Applied Psycholinguistics* 37 (1), 165–193.

Anderson, L.W. and Krathwohl, D.R. (2001) *A Taxonomy for Learning, Teaching and Assessing: A Revision of Bloom's Taxonomy of Educational Objectives*. New York: Longman Publishing.

Annual Report on Immigration (2012) Finnish Immigration Service. See https://migri.fi/etusivu.

Arffman, I. (2013) Problems and issues in translating international educational achievement tests. *Educational Measurement: Issues and Practice* 32 (2), 2–14. doi: https://doi.org/10.1111/emip.12007

Armon-Lotem, S., de Jong, J. and Meir, N. (eds) (2015) *Assessing Multilingual Children: Disentangling Bilingualism from Language Impairment*. Bristol: Multilingual Matters.

Aronin, L. and Singleton, D. (2012) *Multilingualism*. Amsterdam: John Benjamins.

Artiles, A.J., Rueda, R., Salazar, J. and Higareda, I. (2005) Within-group diversity in minority special education disproportionate representation: The case of English language learners in California's urban school districts. *Exceptional Children* 71, 283–300.

ASTAT (n.d.) Provincia Autonoma di Bolzano. Istituto Nazionale di Statistica. See https://astat.provincia.bz.it/it/default.asp.

Baetens Beardsmore, H. (1993) An overview of European models of bilingual education. *Language, Culture and Curriculum* 6 (3), 197–208. doi: 10.1080/07908319309525151

Baird, J., Andrich, D., Hopfenbeck, T.N. and Stobart, G. (2017) Assessment and learning: Fields apart? *Assessment in Education: Principles, Policy and Practice* 24 (3), 317–350. doi: 10.1080/0969594X.2017.1319337

Baker, C. (2001) *Foundations of Bilingual Education and Bilingualism* (3rd edn). Clevedon: Multilingual Matters.

Baker, C. (2006) *Foundations of Bilingual Education and Bilingualism* (4th edn). Clevedon: Multilingual Matters.

Baker, C. and Prys Jones, S. (1998) *Encyclopedia of Bilingualism and Bilingual Education*. Clevedon: Multilingual Matters.

Baker, C. and Wright, W.E. (2017) *Foundations of Bilingual Education and Bilingualism* (6th edn). Bristol: Multilingual Matters.

Bardel, C. and Falk, Y (2007) The role of the second language in third language acquisition: The case of Germanic syntax. *Second Language Research* 23, 459–484.

Bardel, C. and Lindqvist, C. (2007) The role of proficiency and psychotypology in lexical cross-linguistic influence: A study of a multilingual learner of Italian L3. In M. Chini, P. Desideri, M.E. Favilla and G. Pallotti (eds) *Atti del VI Congresso di Studi dell"Associazione Italiana di Linguistica Applicata*, Napoli 9–10 February 2006 (pp. 123–145). Perugia: Guerra Editore.

Beetsma, D. (2002) *Trilingual Primary Education in Europe. Inventory of the Provisions for Trilingual Primary Education in Minority Language Communities of the European Union*. Ljouwert/Leeuwarden: Fryske Akademy/Mercator Education.

Berman, R.A. and Slobin, D.I. (1994) *Relating Events in Narrative: A Cross-Linguistic Developmental Study*. Hillsdale, NJ: Lawrence Erlbaum.

Björklund, S. (1997) Immersion in Finland in the 1990s. In R.K. Johnson and M. Swain (eds) *Immersion Education: International Perspectives* (pp. 85–101). Cambridge: Cambridge University Press.

Björklund, S. and Lasagabaster, D. (2002) Language learning through immersion programmes in Finland. *Journal for the Study of Education and Development* 25 (4), 469–483. doi: 10.1174/021037002762064046

Björklund, S., Mård-Miettinen, K. and Savijärvi, M. (2014) Swedish immersion in the early years in Finland. *International Journal of Bilingual Education and Bilingualism* 17 (2), 197–214. doi: 10.1080/13670050.2013.866628

Bley-Vroman, R. (1983) The comparative fallacy in interlanguage studies: The case of systematicity. *Language Learning* 33, 1–17.

Botting, N. (2002) Narrative as a tool for the assessment of linguistic and pragmatic impairments. *Child Language Teaching and Therapy* 18 (1), 1–21.

Bristol, L. (2015) Leading-for-inclusion: Transforming action through teacher talk. *International Journal of Inclusive Education* 19 (8), 802–820. doi: 10.1080/13603116.2014.971078

Canagarajah, S. (2012) *Translingual Practice: Global Englishes and Cosmopolitan Relations*. London: Routledge. doi: 10.4324/9780203073889

Cenoz, J. (2009) *Towards Multilingual Education: Basque Educational Research from an International Perspective*. Bristol: Multilingual Matters.

Cenoz, J. (2013) The influence of bilingualism on third language acquisition: Focus on multilingualism. *Language Teaching* 46 (1), 71–86. doi: 10.1017/S0261444811000218

Cenoz, J., Hufeisen, B. and Jessner, U. (2001) Towards trilingual education. *International Journal of Bilingual Education and Bilingualism* 4 (1), 1–10. doi: 10.1080/13670050108667714

Cenoz, J., Arozena, E. and Gorter, D. (2013) Assessing multilingual students' writing skills in Basque, Spanish and English. In V.C.M. Gathercole (ed.) *Issues in the Assessment of Bilinguals* (pp. 185–204). Bristol: Multilingual Matters.

Cenoz, J., Genesee, F. and Gorter, D. (2014) Critical analysis of CLIL: Taking stock and looking forward. *Applied Linguistics* 35 (3), 243–262. doi: 10.1093/applin/amt011

Cherryholmes, C.H. (1988) Construct validity and the discourses of research. *American Journal of Education* 96 (3), 421–457.

Clark, E.V. (2016) *First Language Acquisition* (3rd edn). Cambridge: Cambridge University Press.

Cleave, P.L., Girolametto, L.E., Chen, X. and Johnson, C.J. (2010) Narrative abilities in monolingual and dual language learning children with specific language impairment. *Journal of Communication Disorders* 43 (6), 511–522.

Cook, V. (1991) The poverty of the stimulus argument and multicompetence. *Second Language Research* 7 (2), 103–117.

Cook, V. (1992) Evidence for multicompetence. *Language Learning* 42 (4), 557–592.

Cook, V. (1995) Multi-competence and the learning of many languages. *Language, Culture and Curriculum* 8, 93–98.

Cook, V. (1997) Monolingual bias in second language research. *Revista de Estudios Ingleses* 34, 35–50.

Cook, V. (2001) Using the first language in the classroom. *Canadian Modern Language Review* 57 (3), 402–423.

Cook, V. (2015) Premises of multicompetence. In V.J. Cook and Li Wei (eds) *The Cambridge Handbook of Linguistic Multicompetence* (pp. 1–25). Cambridge: Cambridge University Press.

Cook, V. (2016) *Second Language Learning and Language Teaching*. Abingdon: Routledge.

Council of Europe (2018a) *Collated Representative Samples of Language Competences Developed for Young Learners aged 7–10 years*. Resource for Educators, Volume 1. See https://rm.coe.int/collated-representative-samples-descriptors-young-learners-volume-1-ag/16808b1688.

Council of Europe (2018b) *Collated Representative Samples of Language Competences Developed for Young Learners aged 11–15 years*. Resource for Educators, Volume 2. See https://rm.coe.int/collated-representative-samples-descriptors-young-learners-volume-2-ag/16808b1689.

Coyle, D. (2008) CLIL: A pedagogical approach from the European perspective. In N. Van Deusen-Scholl and N. Hornberger (eds) *Encyclopedia of Language and Education* (2nd edn; pp. 97–111). New York: Springer.

Coyle, D., Hood, P. and Marsh, D. (2010) *CLIL Content and Language Integrated Learning*. Cambridge: Cambridge University Press.

Creese, A. and Blackledge, A. (2011) Separate and flexible bilingualism in complementary schools: Multiple language practices in interrelationship. *Journal of Pragmatics* 43 (5), 1196–1208. doi: 10.1016/j.pragma.2010.10.006

Cronbach, L.J. and Meehl, P.E. (1955) Construct validity in psychological tests. *Psychological Bulletin* 52, 281–302.

Crossley, S.A., Salsbury, T., McNamara, D.S. and Jarvis, S. (2011) Predicting lexical proficiency in language learner texts using computational indices. *Language Testing* 28 (4), 561–580. doi: 10.1177/0265532210378031

Cummins, J. (1979) Linguistic interdependence and the educational development of bilingual children. *Review of Educational Research* 49 (2), 222–251. doi: http://dx.doi.org/10.2307/1169960

Cummins, J. (1979a) Cognitive/academic language proficiency, linguistic interdependence, the optimum age question and some other matters. *Working Papers on Bilingualism* 19, 121–129.

Cummins, J. (1979b) Linguistic interdependence and the educational development of bilingual children. *Review of Educational Research* 49 (2), 222–251. doi: https://doi.org/10.3102/00346543049002222

Cummins, J. (1980) Psychological assessment of immigrant children: Logic or intuition? *Journal of Multilingual and Multicultural Development* 1 (2), 97–111. doi: 10.1080/01434632.1980.9994005

Cummins, J. (1981a) The role of primary language development in promoting educational success for language minority students. In California State Department of Education (ed.) *Schooling and Language Minority Students: A Theoretical Framework* (pp. 3–49). Los Angeles, CA: Evaluation, Dissemination and Assessment Center California State University.

Cummins, J. (1981b) Age on arrival and immigrant second language learning in Canada: A reassessment. *Applied Linguistics* 1, 132–149.

Cummins, J. (1984) *Bilingualism and Special Education: Issues in Assessment and Pedagogy*. Clevedon: Multilingual Matters.

Cummins, J. (1998) Rossell and Baker: Their case for the effectiveness of bilingual education. *Journal of Pedagogy, Pluralism, and Practice* 1 (3), 15–20.

Cummins, J. (2008) BICS and CALP: Empirical and theoretical status of the distinction. In B. Street and N.H. Hornberger (eds) *Encyclopedia of Language and Education*, Vol. 2: Literacy (2nd edn; pp. 71–83). New York: Springer Science and Business Media LLC.

Dagenais, D., Armand, F., Walsh, N. and Maraillet, E. (2007) L'Éveil aux langues et la coconstruction de connaissances sur la diversité linguistique. *Canadian Journal of Applied Linguistics* 10 (2), 197–219.

Dalton-Puffer, C., Llinares, A., Lorenzo, F. and Nikula, T. (2014) You can stand under my umbrella: Immersion, CLIL and bilingual education. A response to Cenoz, Genesee and Gorter (2013). *Applied Linguistics* 35 (2), 213–218. doi: https://doi.org/10.1093/applin/amu010

Davis, J.M. (2018) Terminology: Assessment, evaluation, and testing. In C. Coombe and J.D. Brown (eds) *The TESOL Encyclopedia of English Language Teaching*. Hoboken, NJ: Wiley & Sons. doi: 10.1002/9781118784235.eelt0341

De Angelis, G. (2007) *Third or Additional Language Acquisition*. Clevedon: Multilingual Matters.

De Angelis, G. (2012) The effect of population distribution on L1 and L2 acquisition: Evidence from the multilingual region of South Tyrol. *International Journal of Multilingualism* 9 (4), 407–422.

De Angelis, G. (2014) A multilingual approach to analysing standardized test results: Immigrant primary school children and the role of languages spoken in a bi-/multilingual community. *Intercultural Education* 25 (1), 14–28. doi: 10.1080/14675986.2014.883167

De Angelis, G. (2018) Cross-linguistic influence and multiple language acquisition and use. In D. Singleton and L. Aronin (eds) *Twelve Lectures on Multilingualism* (pp. 163–178). Bristol: Multilingual Matters.

De Angelis, G. (2019) The bilingual advantage and the language background bias. *Theory and Practice of Second Language Acquisition* 5 (2), 11–23. doi: https://doi.org/10.31261/tapsla.7554

De Angelis, G. and Selinker, L. (2001) Interlanguage transfer and competing linguistic systems in the multilingual mind. In J. Cenoz, B. Hufeisen and U. Jessner (eds) *Crosslinguistic Influence in Third Language Acquisition: Psycholinguistic Perspectives* (pp. 42–58). Clevedon: Multilingual Matters.

De Angelis, G. and Dewaele, J.-M. (eds) (2011) *New Trends in Crosslinguistic Influence and Multilingualism Research*. Bristol: Multilingual Matters.

De Angelis, G. and Jessner, U. (2012) Writing across languages in a bilingual context: A dynamic systems theory approach. In R.M. Manchón (ed.) *L2 Writing Development: Multiple Perspectives* (pp. 47–68). Berlin: Mouton de Gruyter.

De Backer, F., Van Avermaet, P. and Slembrouck, S. (2017) Schools as laboratories for exploring multilingual assessment policies and practices. *Language and Education* 31 (3), 217–230. doi: 10.1080/09500782.2016.1261896

de Bot, K. (2017) Complexity theory and dynamic systems theory. In L. Ortega and Z. Han (eds) *Complexity Theory and Language Development* (pp. 51–58). Amsterdam/Philadelphia, PA: John Benjamins.

De Houwer, A. (2009) *Bilingual First Language Acquisition*. Bristol: Multilingual Matters.

Dendrinos, B. (2019) Multilingual Testing and Assessment for Plurilingual Education. 'MultiTest' ECSPM position paper. See http://ecspm.org/wp-content/uploads/2019/03/MultiTest.pdf (accessed 8 June 2020).

Dicks, J. and Genesee, F. (2017) Bilingual education in Canada. In O. García, A. Lin and S. May (eds) *Bilingual and Multilingual Education. Encyclopedia of Language and Education* (3rd edn). Cham: Springer. doi: https://doi.org/10.1007/978-3-319-02258-1_32

Doecke, B., Kostogriz, A. and Illesca, B. (2010) Seeing 'things' differently: Recognition, ethics, praxis. *English Teaching: Practice and Critique* 9 (2), 81–98.

Duncan, T.G., Parent, L., Chen, W.-H., Ferrara, S., Johnson, E., Oppler, S. and Shieh, Y.Y. (2005) Study of a dual-language test booklet in eighth-grade mathematics. *Applied Measurement in Education* 18 (2), 129–161. doi: 10.1207/s15324818ame1802_1

Eichinger, L. (2010) South Tyrol: German and Italian in a changing world. *Journal of Multilingual and Multicultural Development* 23 (1–2), 137–149.

Ellis, R. and Shintani, N. (2014) *Exploring Language Pedagogy through Second Language Acquisition Research*. London: Routledge.

Encuesta Sociolinguistica (2011) Comunidad Autónoma del País Vasco, Departamento de Educación, Política Lingüística y Cultura. See https://en.eustat.eus/elementos/ele0012400/V...2011/inf0012423_i.pdf

Ercikan, K. (1998) Translation effects in international assessments. *International Journal of Educational Research* 29 (6), 543–553.

Escamilla, K., Mahon, E., Riley-Bernal, H. and Rutledge, D. (2003) High-stakes testing, Latinos, and English language learners: Lessons from Colorado. *Bilingual Research Journal* 27 (1), 25–49. doi: 10.1080/15235882.2003.10162590

Escamilla, K., Hopewell, S., Butvilofsky, S., Sparrow, W., Soltero-Gonzalez, L., Ruiz-Figueroa, O. and Escamilla, M. (2014) *Biliteracy from the Start: Literacy Squared in Action*. Philadelphia, PA: Caslon Publishing.

Escamilla, K., Butvilofsky, S. and Hopewell, S. (2018) What gets lost when English-only writing assessment is used to assess writing proficiency in Spanish-English emerging bilingual learners? *International Multilingual Research Journal* 12 (4), 221–236. doi: 10.1080/19313152.2016.1273740

Etxeberria, F. and Elosegi, K. (2008) Basque, Spanish and immigrant minority languages in Basque schools. *Language, Culture and Curriculum* 21 (1), 69–84. doi: 10.2167/lcc344.0

Eurostat (2019) Foreign language learning statistics. See https://ec.europa.eu/eurostat/statistics-explained/pdfscache/1151.pdf

Eurydice (2006) Content and Language Integrated Learning (CLIL) at School in Europe. Eurydice at NFER. See http://www.nfer.ac.uk/shadomx/apps/fms/fmsdownload.cfm?file_uuid=A9819C1B-C29E-AD4D-03A8-58D5CCC7A219andsiteName=nfer (accessed March 23).

Fairbairn, S.B. and Fox, J. (2009) Inclusive achievement testing for linguistically and culturally diverse test takers: Essential considerations for test developers and decision makers. *Educational Measurement: Issues and Practice* 28, 10–24. doi: 10.1111/j.1745-3992.2009.01133.x

Fiestas, C.E. and Peña, E.D. (2004) Narrative discourse in bilingual children: Language and task effects. *Language, Speech, and Hearing Services in Schools* 35 (2), 155–168.

Flynn, S., Foley, C. and Vinnitskaya, I. (2004) The cumulative-enhancement model for language acquisition: Comparing adults' and children's patterns of development in first, second and third language acquisition of relative clauses. *International Journal of Multilingualism* 1 (1), 3–16. doi: 10.1080/14790710408668175

Fox, J. and Cheng, L. (2007) Did we take the same test? Differing accounts of the Ontario Secondary School Literacy Test by first and second language test-takers. *Assessment in Education: Principles, Policy and Practice* 14 (1), 9–26. doi: 10.1080/09695940701272773

Gagarina, N., Klop, D., Kunnari, S., Tantele, K., Välimaa, T., Balčiūnienė, I., Bohnacker, U. and Walters, J. (2012) Part I. MAIN: Multilingual assessment instrument for narratives. *ZAS Papers in Linguistics* 56, 1–139. See http://195.37.93.18/fileadmin/material/ZASPiL_Volltexte/zp56/MAIN_English_corrected.pdf (accessed 23 May 2019).

Gandara, F. and Randall, J. (2019) Assessing mathematics proficiency of multilingual students: The case for translanguaging in the Democratic Republic of Congo. *Comparative Education Review* 63 (1), 58–78.

García, O. (2009) *Bilingual Education in the 21st Century. A Global Perspective*. Malden, MA: Wiley-Blackwell.

García, O. and Li Wei (2014) *Translanguaging: Language, Bilingualism and Education*. Basingstoke: Palgrave Macmillan.

Gass, S. and Selinker, L. (2008) *Second Language Acquisition: An Introductory Course*. New York: Routledge.

Gathercole, V.C.M., Thomas, E.M., Roberts, E.J., Hughes, C.O. and Hughes E.K. (2013) Why assessment needs to take exposure into account: Vocabulary and grammatical abilities in bilingual children. In V.C.M. Gathercole (ed.) *Issues in the Assessment of Bilinguals* (pp. 20–55). Bristol: Multilingual Matters.

Gierl, M. (2000) Construct equivalence on translated achievement tests. *Canadian Journal of Education Revue Canadienne De L'éducation* 25 (4), 280–296. doi: 10.2307/1585851

Gonzalez, V. (2012) Assessment of bilingual/multilingual pre-k–grade 12 students: A critical discussion of past, present, and future issue. *Theory into Practice* 51 (4), 290–296. doi: 10.1080/00405841.2012.726058

Gorter, D. and Cenoz, J. (2017) Language education policy and multilingual assessment. *Language and Education* 31 (3), 231–248. doi: 10.1080/09500782.2016.1261892

Green, E.J. (1997) Guidelines for serving linguistically and culturally diverse young children. *Early Childhood Education Journal* 24, 147–154. doi: https://doi.org/10.1007/BF02353271

Grosjean, F. (1985) The bilingual as a competent but specific speaker-hearer. *Journal of Multilingual and Multicultural Development* 6 (6), 467–477.

Grosjean, F. (1989) Neurolinguists, beware! The bilingual is not two monolinguals in one person. *Brain Language* 36 (1), 3–15. doi: 10.1016/0093-934X(89)90048-5

Grosjean, F. (1992) Another view of bilingualism. In R.J. Harris (ed.) *Cognitive Processing in Bilinguals* (pp. 51–62). Amsterdam: North Holland.

Grosjean, F. (2001) The bilingual's language modes. In J.L. Nicol (ed.) *One Mind, Two Languages: Bilingual Language Processing* (pp. 1–22). Oxford: Blackwell.

Gutiérrez, K.D., Baquedano-López, P., Alvarez, H.H. and Chiu, M.M. (1999) Building a culture of collaboration through hybrid language practices. *Theory into Practice* 38 (2), 87–93. doi: 10.1080/00405849909543837

Gutiérrez-Clellen, V.F. (2002) Narratives in two languages: Assessing performance of bilingual children. *Linguistics and Education* 13 (2), 175–197.

Gutierrez-Clellen, V.F., Simon-Cereijido, G. and Wagner, C. (2008) Bilingual children with language impairment: A comparison with monolinguals and second language learners. *Applied Psycholinguistics* 29, 3–20.

Haag, N., Heppt, B., Stanat, P., Kuhl, P. and Pant, H.A. (2013) Second language learners' performance in mathematics: Disentangling the effects of academic language features. *Learning and Instruction* 28, 24–34.

Hakuta, K., Butler, Y.G. and Witt, D. (2000) How Long Does It Take English Learners to Attain Proficiency? Policy Report 2000-1. The University of California Linguistic Minority Research Institute. https://files.eric.ed.gov/fulltext/ED443275.pdf

Hambleton, R.K. (2001) The next generation of the ITC test translation and adaptation guidelines. *European Journal of Psychological Assessment* 17 (3), 164–172. doi: https://doi.org/10.1027//1015-5759.17.3.164

Hambleton, R.K., Merenda, P.F. and Spielberger, C.D. (2004) *Adapting Educational and Psychological Tests for Cross-Cultural Assessment*. New York: Psychology Press.

Harlen, W. and James, M. (1997) Assessment and learning: Differences and relationships between formative and summative assessment. *Assessment in Education: Principles, Policy and Practice* 4 (3), 365–379. doi: 10.1080/0969594970040304

Heilmann, J., Miller, J.F. and Nockerts, A. (2010) Sensitivity of narrative organization measures using narrative retells produced by young school-age children. *Language Testing* 27, 603–626.

Henn-Reinke, K. (2012) *Considering Trilingual Education*. New York: Routledge. doi: https://doi.org/10.4324/9780203124963

Heppt, B., Haag, N., Böhme, K. and Stanat, P. (2014) The role of academic-language features for reading comprehension of language-minority students and students from low-SES families. *Reading Research Quarterly* 50 (1), 61–82. doi: 10.1002/rrq.83

Herdina, P. and Jessner, U. (2002) *A Dynamic Model of Multilingualism: Perspectives of Change in Psycholinguistics*. Clevedon: Multilingual Matters.

Herzog-Punzenberger, B., Le Pichon-Vorstman, E. and Siarova, H. (2017) Multilingual Education in the Light of Diversity: Lessons Learned. NESET II Report. Publications Office of the European Union, Luxembourg. doi: 10.2766/71255

Heugh, K. (2011) Theory and practice – language education models in Africa: Research, design, decision-making and outcomes. In A. Ouane and C. Glanz (eds) *Optimising Learning, Education and Publishing in Africa: The Language Factor. A Review and Analysis of Theory and Practice in Mother-Tongue and Bilingual Education in Sub-Saharan Africa* (pp. 105–156). Hamburg/Tunis Belvédère: UNESCO Institute for Lifelong Learning (UIL) and the Association for the Development of Education in Africa (ADEA)/African Development Bank. http://unesdoc.unesco.org/images/0021/002126/212602e.pdf

Hipfner-Boucher, K., Milburn, T., Weitzman, E., Greenberg, J., Pelletier, J. and Girolametto, L. (2014) Narrative abilities in subgroups of English language learners and monolingual peers. *International Journal of Bilingualism* 19 (6), 677–692.

Hönig, I. (2010) *Assessment in CLIL: Theoretical and Empirical Research*. Saarbrücken: VDM Verlag Dr. Müller.

Hopewell, S. and Escamilla, K. (2014) Biliteracy development in immersion contexts. *Journal of Immersion and Content-Based Language Education* 2 (2), 181–195.

Hurajovà, A. (2015) An overview of models of bilingual education. *Mediterranean Journal of Social Sciences* 6 (6 S1), 186.

Hutson-Nechkash, P. (1990) *Storybuilding. A Guide to Structuring Oral Narratives*. Eau Claire, WI: Thinking Publications.

Iluz-Cohen, P. and Walters, J. (2012) Telling stories in two languages: Narratives of bilingual preschool children with typical and impaired language. *Bilingualism: Language and Cognition* 15, 58–74.

Instituto Vasco de Estadística (n.d.) See https://en.eustat.eus/indice.html

International Test Commission (2018) ITC guidelines for translating and adapting tests (second edition). *International Journal of Testing* 18 (2), 101–134. doi: 10.1080/15305058.2017.1398166

International Test Commission (2019) ITC guidelines for the large-scale assessment of linguistically and culturally diverse populations. *International Journal of Testing* 19 (4), 301–336. doi: 10.1080/15305058.2019.1631024

INVALSI (2010) *Rapporto_SNV_2009/10. Rilevazione degli apprendimenti*. Servizio Nazionale di Valutazione. See https://www.invalsi.it/invalsi/index.php (accessed 8 March 2020).

ISEI-IVEI (2012) *PISA-L Investigacion sobre la influencia de la lengua de la prueba en las evaluaciones Internacionales. Resultado del alumnado de programas de educación bilingue.* Modelo D. See http://www.isei-ivei.net/cast/pub/PISA-L/PISA-L-final.pdf.

Jacobs, H.L., Zingraf, S.A., Wormuth, D.R., Hartfiel, V.F. and Hughey, J.B. (1981) *Testing ESL Composition*. Rowley, MA: Newbury House.

Jacquemet, M. (2005) Transidiomatic practices: Language and power in the age of globalization. *Language and Communication* 25 (3), 257–277.

Jarvis, S. and Pavlenko, A. (2008) *Cross-Linguistic Influence in Language and Cognition*. New York: Routledge.

Johnson, E. and Monroe, B. (2004) Simplified language as an accommodation on math tests. *Assessment for Effective Intervention* 29 (3), 35–45. doi: https://doi.org/10.1177/073724770402900303

Jørgensen, J. (2008) Polylingual languaging around and among children and adolescents. *International Journal of Multilingualism* 5 (3), 161–176. doi: 10.1080/14790710802387562

Justice, L.M., Bowles, R.P., Kaderavek, J.N., Ukrainetz, T.A., Eisenberg, S.L. and Gillam, R.B. (2006) The index of narrative microstructure: A clinical tool for analyzing school-age children's narrative performances. *American Journal of Speech-Language Pathology* 15 (2), 177–191.

Kachru, Y. (1994) Monolingual bias in SLA research. *TESOL Quarterly* 28 (4), 795–800. doi: 10.2307/3587564

Kagan, O., Carreira, M. and Hitchens Chik, C. (eds) (2017) *The Routledge Handbook of Heritage Language Education*. New York: Routledge. doi: https://doi.org/10.4324/9781315727974

Kieffer, M.J., Lesaux, N.K., Rivera, M. and Francis, D.J. (2009) Accommodations for English language learners taking large-scale assessments: A meta-analysis on effectiveness and validity. *Review of Educational Research* 79 (3), 1168–1201. doi: https://doi.org/10.3102/0034654309332490

Kim, S.H.O. and Elder, C. (2005) Language choices and pedagogic functions in the foreign language classroom: A cross-linguistic functional analysis of teacher talk. *Language Teaching Research* 9 (4), 355–380. doi: https://doi.org/10.1191/1362168805lr173oa

Kramsch, C. (2012) Authenticity and legitimacy in multilingual SLA. *Critical Multilingualism Studies* 1, 107–128.

Krathwohl, D.R. (2002) A revision of Bloom's taxonomy: An overview. *Theory into Practice* 41 (4), 212–218. doi: 10.1207/s15430421tip4104_2

Kupiainen, S., Hautamäki, J. and Karjalainen, T. (2009) *Julkaisusarja*. Ministry of Education Publications, Finland. See https://julkaisut.valtioneuvosto.fi/handle/10024/75640 (accessed 4 August 2020).

Lambert, W.E. (1975) Culture and language as factors in learning and education. In A. Wolfgang (ed.) *Education of Immigrant Students* (pp. 55–83). Toronto: Ontario Institute for Studies in Education.

Larsen-Freeman, D. (1997) Chaos/complexity science and second language acquisition. *Applied Linguistics* 18 (2), 141–165. doi:10.1093/applin/18.2.141

Larsen-Freeman, D. (2011) A complexity theory approach to second language development/acquisition. In D. Atkinson (ed.) *Alternative Approaches to Second Language Acquisition* (pp. 48–72). New York: Routledge.

Lasagabaster, D. (2000a) Three languages and three linguistic models in the Basque educational system. In J. Cenoz and U. Jessner (eds) *English in Europe: The Acquisition of a Third Language* (pp. 179–197). Clevedon: Multilingual Matters.

Lasagabaster, D. (2000b) The effects of three bilingual education models on linguistic creativity. *IRAL, International Review of Applied Linguistics in Language Teaching* 38, 55–70.

Lasagabaster, D. (2001) Bilingualism, immersion programmes and language learning in the Basque Country. *Journal of Multilingual and Multicultural Development* 22, 401–425.

Lasagabaster, D. and Sierra, J.M. (2009) Immersion and CLIL in English: More differences than similarities. *ELT Journal* 63 (4), 367–375. doi: 10.1093/elt/ccp082

Latomaa, S. and Nuolijärvi, P. (2005) The language situation in Finland. In R.B. Kaplan and R.B. Baldauf Jr (eds) *Language Planning and Policy in Europe. Hungary, Finland and Sweden* (Vol. 1; pp. 125–232). Clevedon: Multilingual Matters.

Lever, R. and Sénéchal, M. (2011) Discussing stories: On how a dialogic reading intervention improves kindergartners' oral narrative construction. *Journal of Experimental Child Psychology* 108 (1), 1–24.

Levin, T. and Shohamy, E. (2008) Achievement of immigrant students in mathematics and academic Hebrew in Israeli school: A large-scale evaluation study. *Studies in Educational Evaluation* 34 (1), 1–14. doi: doi.org/10.1016/j.stueduc.2008.01.001

Liles, B. (1993) Narrative discourse in children with language disorders and children with normal language: A critical review of the literature. *Journal of Speech and Hearing Research* 36 (5), 868–882.

Liles, B.Z., Duffy, R.J., Merritt, D.D. and Purcell, S.L. (1995) Measurement of narrative discourse ability in children with language disorders. *Journal of Speech and Hearing Research* 38, 415–425.

Lindholm-Leary, K.J. and Block, N. (2010) Achievement in predominantly low SES/Hispanic dual language schools. *International Journal of Bilingual Education and Bilingualism* 13, 43–60.

Lissón, P. and Ballier, N. (2018) Investigating lexical progression through lexical diversity metrics in a corpus of French L3. *Discours* 23. See https://journals.openedition.org/discours/9950 (accessed 4 July 2019). doi: 10.4000/discours.9950

Lo, Y.Y. and Fung, D. (2018) Assessments in CLIL: The interplay between cognitive and linguistic demands and their progression in secondary education. *International Journal of Bilingual Education and Bilingualism* 1–19. doi: 10.1080/13670050.2018.1436519

López, A.A., Turkan, S. and Guzman-Orth, D. (2016) Assessing multilingual competence. In E. Shohamy, I.G. Or and S. May (eds) *Language Testing and Assessment* (pp. 1–12). Cham: Springer International Publishing. doi: 10.1007/978-3-319-02326-7_6-1

López, A.A., Turkan, S. and Guzman-Orth, D. (2017) Conceptualizing the Use of Translanguaging in Initial Content Assessments for Newly Arrived Emergent Bilingual Students. Research Report No. RR-17-07. Educational Testing Service, Princeton, NJ. doi: http://dx.doi.org/10.1002/ets2.12140

López, A.A., Guzman-Orth, D. and Turkan, S. (2019) Exploring the use of translanguaging to measure the mathematics knowledge of emergent bilingual students. *Translation and Translanguaging in Multilingual Contexts* 5 (2), 143–164.

Lust, B.C. and Foley, C. (eds) (2004) *First Language Acquisition: The Essential Readings*. Malden, MA, Oxford: Blackwell.

Makoni, S. and Pennycook, A. (2012) Disinventing multilingualism: From monological multilingualism to multilingua francas. In M. Martin-Jones, A. Blackledge and A. Creese (eds) *The Routledge Handbook of Multilingualism* (pp. 439–453). New York: Routledge.

Martiniello, M. (2008) Language and the performance of English-language learners in math word problems. *Harvard Education Review* 78 (2), 333–368.

Massler, U., Stotz, D. and Queisser, C. (2014) Assessment instruments for primary CLIL: The conceptualisation and evaluation of test tasks. *The Language Learning Journal* 42 (2), 137–150. doi: 10.1080/09571736.2014.891371

Maxwell, B. (1996) Translation and cultural adaptation of the survey instruments. In M.O. Martin and D.L. Kelly (eds) *Third International Mathematics and Science Study (TIMSS) Technical Report. Volume I: Design and Development* (pp. 8.1–8.10). Chestnut Hill, MA: Boston College. See https://timssandpirls.bc.edu/timss1995i/TIMSSPDF/TRCHP8.pdf

May, S. (ed.) (2014) *The Multilingual Turn: Implications for SLA, TESOL and Bilingual Education*. London/New York: Routledge.

Mayer, M. (1969) *Frog, Where Are You?* New York: Dial Books for Young Readers.
Mayer, M. and Mayer, M. (1975) *One Frog Too Many*. New York: Dial Press.
McLaughlin, M. (2016) Linguistic minorities and the multilingual turn: Constructing language ownership through affect in cultural production. *Multilingua: Journal of Cross-Cultural and Interlanguage Communication* 35 (4), 393–414.
Mehisto, P., Marsh, D. and Frigols, M.J. (2008) *Uncovering CLIL: Content and Language Integrated Learning in Bilingual and Multilingual Education*. Oxford: Macmillan.
Menken, K. (2008) *English Learners Left Behind: Standardized Testing as Language Policy*. Clevedon: Multilingual Matters.
Mercator (2011) *Trilingual Primary Education in Europe*. Mercator European Research Centre on Multilingualism and Language Learning. See www.mercator-research.eu.
Merino, J.A. and Lasagabaster, D. (2018) CLIL as a way to multilingualism. *International Journal of Bilingual Education and Bilingualism* 21 (1), 79–92. doi: 10.1080/13670050.2015.1128386
Meschi, E., Micklewright, J., Vignoles, A. and Lindsay, G. (2012) The Transitions between Categories of Special Educational Needs of Pupils with Speech, Language and Communication Needs (SLCN) and Autism Spectrum Disorder (ASD) as They Progress Through the Education System. London: Department for Education. See http://dera.ioe.ac.uk/16320/1/DFE-RR247-BCRP11.pdf
Milani, T. (2008) Language testing and citizenship: A language ideological debate in Sweden. *Language in Society* 37 (1), 27–59. http://www.jstor.org/stable/20108095
Mitchell, R., Myles, F. and Marsden, E. (2013) *Second Language Learning Theories* (3rd edn). Abingdon: Routledge
Montanari, S. (2004) The development of narrative competence in the L1 and L2 of Spanish-English bilingual children. *International Journal of Bilingualism* 8 (4), 449–497. doi: https://doi.org/10.1177/13670069040080040301
Mori, Y. and Calder, T.M. (2013) Bilingual vocabulary knowledge and arrival age among Japanese heritage language students at Hoshuukoo. *Foreign Language Annals* 46 (2), 290–310.
Myles, F. (2010) The development of theories of second language acquisition. *Language Teaching* 43, 320–332. doi: 10.1017/S0261444810000078
Nortvedt, G.A., Wiese, E., Brown, M., Burns, D., McNamara, G., O'Hara, J., Altrichter, H., Fellner, M., Herzog-Punzenberger, B., Nayir, F. and Taneri, P.O. (2020) Aiding culturally responsive assessment in schools in a globalising world. *Educational Assessment, Evaluation and Accountability* 32, 5–27. doi: https://doi.org/10.1007/s11092-020-09316-w
OECD (2010) *TALIS 2008 Technical Report*. Paris: TALIS, OECD Publishing. doi: https://doi.org/10.1787/9789264079861-en
OECD (2012) *PISA 2009 Technical Report*. Paris: PISA, OECD Publishing. doi: https://doi.org/10.1787/9789264167872-en
OECD (2018) *PISA 2018 Translation and Adaptation Guidelines*. See https://www.oecd.org/pisa/pisaproducts/PISA-2018-TRANSLATION-AND-ADAPTATION-GUIDELINES.pdf
Ong, S.L. (2013) Usefulness of dual-language science test for bilingual learners. *Studies in Educational Evaluation* 39 (2), 82–89.
Ortega, L. (2013) SLA for the 21st century: Disciplinary progress, transdisciplinary relevance, and the bi/multilingual turn. *Language Learning* 63 (1), 1–24.
Ortiz, S.O., Ochoa, S.H. and Dynda, A.M. (2012) Testing with culturally and linguistically diverse populations: Moving beyond the verbal-performance dichotomy into evidence-based practice. In D.P. Flanagan and P.L. Harrison (eds) *Contemporary Intellectual Assessment: Theories, Tests, and Issues* (pp. 526–552). London: The Guilford Press.
Otheguy, R., García, O. and Reid, W. (2015) Clarifying translanguaging and deconstructing named languages: A perspective from linguistics. *Applied Linguistics Review* 6 (3), 281–307. doi: 10.1515/applirev-2015-0014

Otsuji, E. and Pennycook, A. (2010) Metrolingualism: Fixity, fluidity and language in flux. *International Journal of Multilingualism* 7 (3), 240–254. doi: 10.1080/14790710903414331

Otto, A. and Estrada, J.L. (2019) Towards an understanding of CLIL in a European context: Main assessment tools and the role of language in content subjects. *CLIL Journal of Innovation and Research in Plurilingual and Pluricultural Education* 2 (1), 31–42. doi: https:// doi.org/10.5565/rev/clil.11

Pankratz, M.E., Plante, E., Vance, R. and Iinsalaco, D.M. (2007) The diagnostic and predictive validity of The Renfrew Bus story. *Language, Speech, and Hearing Services in Schools* 38 (4), 390–399.

Pearson, B.Z. (2002) Narrative competence among monolingual and bilingual school children in Miami. In D.K. Oller and R.E. Eilers (eds) *Language and Literacy in Bilingual Children* (pp. 135–174). Clevedon: Multilingual Matters.

Pitoniak, M.J. and Royer, J.M. (2001) Testing Accommodations for examinees with disabilities: A review of psychometric, legal, and social policy issues. *Review of Educational Research* 71 (1), 53–104. doi: https://doi.org/10.3102/00346543071001053

Potowski, K. and Muñoz-Basols, J. (eds) (2018) *The Routledge Handbook of Spanish as a Heritage Language*. Abingdon: Routledge.

Poza, L. (2017) Translanguaging: Definitions, implications, and further needs in burgeoning inquiry. *Berkeley Review of Education* 6 (2), 101–128. doi: http://dx.doi.org/10.5070/B86110060

Puig-Mayenco, E., González Alonso, J. and Rothman, J. (2020) A systematic review of transfer studies in third language acquisition. *Second Language Research* 36 (1), 31–64. doi: https://doi.org/10.1177/0267658318809147

Rasom, O. (2010) CLIL: una chance per la promozione delle lingue minoritarie? Paper presented at IV Giornate dei Diritti Linguistici, 20–23 May, Teramo, Italy.

Rast, R. (2010) The use of prior linguistic knowledge in the early stages of L3 acquisition. *IRAL, International Review of Applied Linguistics in Language Teaching* 48, 159–183.

Rautalin, M. (2018) PISA and the criticism of Finnish education: Justifications used in the national media debate. *Studies in Higher Education* 43 (10), 1778–1791. doi: 10.1080/03075079.2018.1526773

Reese, E., Sparks, A. and Suggate, S. (2012) Assessing children's narratives. In E. Hoff (ed.) *Research Methods in Child Language* (pp. 133–148). Chichester: Wiley Blackwell Ltd.

Regione Autonoma Valle d'Aosta (n.d.) Statistics. See https://www.regione.vda.it/statistica/.

Renfrew, C. (1969) *The Bus Story: A Test of Continuous Speech*. Headington: Renfrew.

Rhodes, R.L., Ochoa, S.H. and Ortiz, S.O. (2005) *Assessing Culturally and Linguistically Diverse Students. A Practical Guide*. New York: The Guildford Press.

Richards, J. and Rodgers, T. (2001) *Approaches and Methods in Language Teaching*. Cambridge: Cambridge University Press.

Ringbom, H. (2007) *Cross-linguistic Similarity in Foreign Language Learning*. Clevedon: Multilingual Matters.

Rix, J. (2009) A model of simplification: The ways in which teachers simplify learning materials, *Educational Studies* 35 (2), 95–106. doi: 10.1080/03055690802470290

Robinson, J.P. (2010) The effects of test translation on young English learners' mathematics performance. *Educational Researcher* 39 (8), 582–590.

Roch, M., Florit, E. and Levorato, C. (2016) Narrative competence of Italian–English bilingual children between 5 and 7 years. *Applied Psycholinguistics* 37 (1), 49–67.

Rossell, C.H. and Baker, K. (1996) The educational effectiveness of bilingual education. *Research in the Teaching of English* 30 (1), 7–74.

Rumelhart, D.E. (1975) Notes on a schema for stories. In D.G. Brown and A. Collins (eds) *Representation and Understanding: Studies in Cognitive Science* (pp. 211–236). New York: Academic Press.

Salkind, N.J. (2010) *Encyclopedia of Research Design* (Vols. 1-0). Thousand Oaks, CA: Sage Publications. doi: 10.4135/9781412961288

Samson, J.F. and Lesaux, N.K. (2009) Language-minority learners in special education: Rates and predictors of identification for services. *Journal of Learning Disabilities* 42 (2), 148–162. doi: https://doi.org/10.1177/0022219408326221

Sanchez, S.V., Rodriguez, B.J., Soto-Huerta, M.E., Castro Villareal, F., Guerra, N.S. and Bustos Flores, B. (2013) A case for multidimensional bilingual assessment. *Language Assessment Quarterly* 10, 160–177.

Saville-Troike, M. and Barto, K. (2017) *Introducing Second Language Acquisition*. Cambridge: Cambridge University Press.

Schissel, J.L. (2014) Classroom use of test accommodations: Issues of access, equity, and conflation. *Current Issues in Language Planning* 15 (3), 282–295. doi: 10.1080/14664208.2014.915458

Schneider, P. (1996) Effects of pictures versus orally presented stories on story retellings by children with language impairment. *American Journal of Speech-Language Pathology* 5 (1), 86–96.

Schneider, P., Hayward, D. and Dubé, R.V. (2006) Storytelling from pictures using the Edmonton Narrative Norms Instrument. *Journal of Speech-Language Pathology and Audiology* 30 (4), 224–238.

Sembiante, S. (2016) Translanguaging and the multilingual turn: Epistemological reconceptualization in the fields of language and implications for reframing language in curriculum studies. *Curriculum Inquiry* 46 (1), 45–61. doi: 10.1080/03626784.2015.1133221

Shaw, S.D. and Imam, H.C. (2013) Assessment of international students through the medium of English: Ensuring validity and fairness in content-based examinations. *Language Assessment Quarterly* 10 (4), 452–475.

Shen, J. and Cooley, V. (2008) Critical issues in using data for decision-making. *International Journal of Leadership in Education* 11 (3), 319–329.

Shohamy, E. (2007) Language tests as language policy tools. *Assessment in Education* 14 (1), 117–130. doi: 10.1080/09695940701272948

Shohamy, E. (2011) Assessing multilingual competencies: Adopting construct valid assessment policies. *The Modern Language Journal* 95, 418–429. doi: 10.1111/j.1540-4781.2011.01210.x

Shohamy, E. and Menken, K. (2015) Language assessment. In W.E. Wright, S. Boun and O. García (eds) *The Handbook of Bilingual and Multilingual Education* (pp. 253–269). Hoboken, NJ: John Wiley and Sons.

Sierens, S. and Van Avermaet, P. (2014) Language diversity in education: Evolving from multilingual education to functional multilingual learning. In D. Little, C. Leung and P. Van Avermaet (eds) *Managing Diversity in Education: Languages, Policies, Pedagogies* (pp. 204–222). Bristol: Multilingual Matters.

Sierra, J. (2008) Assessment of bilingual education in the Basque Country. *Language, Culture and Curriculum* 21 (1), 39–47. doi: 10.2167/lcc341.0

Sireci, S.G., Scarpati, S.E. and Li, S. (2005) Test accommodations for students with disabilities: An analysis of the Interaction Hypothesis. *Review of Educational Research* 75 (4), 457–490. doi: https://doi.org/10.3102/00346543075004457

Solano-Flores, G., Wang, C. and Shade, C. (2016) International semiotics: Item difficulty and the complexity of science item illustrations in the PISA-2009 international test comparison. *International Journal of Testing* 16 (3), 205–219. doi: 10.1080/15305058.2015.1099534

Soltero-González, L., Sparrow, W., Butvilofsky, S., Escamilla, K. and Hopewell, S. (2016) Effects of a paired literacy program on emerging bilingual children's biliteracy outcomes in third grade. *Journal of Literacy Research* 48 (1), 80–104. doi: https://doi.org/10.1177/1086296X16653842

Squires, K.E., Lugo-Neris, M.J., Peña, E.D., Bedore, L.M., Bohman, T.M. and Gillam, R.B. (2014) Story retelling by bilingual children with language impairments and typically developing controls. *International Journal of Language and Communication Disorders* 49 (1), 60–74.

SREV (2010) *Le competenze bilingui degli studenti valdostani.* Struttura Regionale per la Valutazione del sistema scolastico della Valle d'Aosta. See https://www.regione.vda.it/istruzione/SREV/pubblicazioni_i.asp

SREV (2019) *Memento statistico della scuola valdostana N. 15.* Struttura Regionale per la Valutazione del sistema scolastico della Valle d'Aosta. https://www.regione.vda.it/istruzione/SREV/pubblicazioni_i.asp

Stansfield, C.W. (2011) Oral Translation as a test accommodation for ELLs. *Language Testing* 28 (3), 401–416.

Statistics Finland (n.d.) See https://www.stat.fi/index_en.html.

Stavans, A. and Hoffmann, C. (2015) *Multilingualism.* Cambridge: Cambridge University Press.

Stein, N. and Glenn, G. (1975) An analysis of story comprehension in elementary school children. In R. Freedle (ed.) *New Directions in Discourse Processing* (pp. 53–120). Norwood, NJ: Ablex.

Stevens, D.D. and Levi, A. (2013) *Introduction to Rubrics: An Assessment Tool to Save Grading Time, Convey Effective Feedback, and Promote Student Learning* (2nd edn). Sterling, VI: Stylus Publications.

Strauss, M.E. and Smith, G.T. (2009) Construct validity: Advances in theory and methodology. *Annual Review of Clinical Psychology* 5, 1–25. doi: https://doi.org/10.1146/annurev.clinpsy.032408.153639

Sullivan, A.L., A'Vant, E., Baker, J., Chandler, D., Graves, S., McKinney, E. and Sayles, T. (2009) Promising practices in addressing disproportionality. *NASP Communiqué* 38 (2), 18–20.

Svonni, M. (2001) *The Sámi Language in Education in Sweden.* Mercator Working Papers. Leeuwarden: Mercator-Education.

Swain, M. (2000) French immersion research in Canada: Recent contributions to SLA and Applied Linguistics. *Annual Review of Applied Linguistics* 20, 199–212. doi: 10.1017/S0267190500200123

Takahashi-Breines, H. (2002) The role of teacher-talk in a dual language immersion third grade classroom. *Bilingual Research Journal* 26 (2), 461–483. doi: 10.1080/15235882.2002.10668721

Thomas, W. and Collier, V. (2002) *A National Study of School Effectiveness for Language Minority Students' Long-Term Academic Achievement: Final Report. Project 1.1.* Santa Cruz, CA: Center for Research on Education, Diversity and Excellence (CREDE).

Trabasso, T. and Nickels, M. (1992) The development of goal plans of action in the narration of a picture story. *Discourse Processes* 15 (3), 249–275. doi: https://doi-org.elib.tcd.ie/10.1080/01638539209544812

Turkan, S. and Oliveri, M.E. (2014) Considerations for Providing Test Translation Accommodations to English Language Learners on Common Core Standards-Based Assessments. Research Report. ETS RR-14-05. Educational Testing Service, Princeton, NJ. doi: 10.1002/ets2.12003

Uccelli, P. and Páez, M. (2007) Narrative and vocabulary development of bilingual children from kindergarten to first grade: Developmental changes and associations among English and Spanish skills. *Language, Speech, and Hearing Services in Schools* 38 (3), 225–236.

Unsworth, S. (2016) Quantity and quality of language input in bilingual language development. In E. Nicoladis and S. Montanari (eds) *Bilingualism across the Lifespan: Factors Moderating Language Proficiency* (pp. 103–121). Washington, DC: American Psychological Association. doi: https://doi-org.elib.tcd.ie/10.1037/14939-007

Upsing, B. and Rittberger, M. (2018) The translator's perspective on translation quality control processes for international large-scale assessment studies. *Translation and Interpreting* 10 (2), 55–72.

Van der Schaaf, A. and Verra, R. (2001) *The Ladin Language Education in Italy*. Leeuwarden: Mercator-Education.

Vance, N. (2019) *Bilingual Education*. Salem Press Encyclopedia.

Vernetto, G. (2019) Competenze linguistiche e competenze plurilingui: quali strumenti per la valutazione e la valorizzazione? Paper presented at the Dille Conference in Malta, 23–24 May.

Wang, L. and Kirkpatrick, A. (2019) *Trilingual Education in Hong Kong*. Cham: Springer.

Westby, C. (1984) Development of narrative language abilities. In G. Wallach and K. Butler (eds) *Language Learning Disabilities in School-Age Children* (pp. 103–127). Baltimore, MD: Williams and Wilkins.

Westby, C. (2005) Assessing and facilitating text comprehension problems. In H. Catts and A. Kamhi (eds) *Language and Reading Disabilities* (2nd edn, pp. 157–232). Boston, MA: Allyn and Bacon.

Westerveld, M.F. and Vidler, K. (2015) The use of the Renfrew Bus Story with 5–8-year-old Australian children. *International Journal of Speech-Language Pathology* 17 (3), 304–313. doi: 10.3109/17549507.2015.1024168

Willner, L.S. and Mokhtari, K. (2017) Improving meaningful use of accommodations by multilingual learners. *The Reading Teacher* 71 (4), 431–439.

Wolfe-Quintero, K., Shunji, I. and Hae-Young, K. (1998) *Second Language Development in Writing: Measures of Fluency, Accuracy and Complexity*. Honolulu, HI: University of Hawaii Press.

Woodcock, G. (1992) The new Autonomy Statute of Trentino-Alto Adige (the end of the South Tyrol question). *Il Politico* 57 (1), 127–145.

Wright, W.E. and Li, X. (2008) High-stakes math tests: How No Child Left Behind leaves newcomer English language learners behind. *Language Policy* 7 (3), 237–266. doi: 10.1007/s10993-008-9099-2

Young, J.W., Cho, Y., Ling, G., Cline, F., Steinberg, J. and Stone, E. (2008) Validity and fairness of state standards-based assessments for English language learners. *Educational Assessment* 13 (2–3), 170–192.

Young, V.A. and Martinez, A.Y. (2011) *Code-Meshing as World English: Pedagogy, Policy, Performance*. Urbana, IL: National Council of Teachers of English.

Ytsma, J. (2001) Towards a typology of trilingual primary education. *International Journal of Bilingual Education and Bilingualism* 4 (1), 11–22. doi: 10.1080/13670050108667715

Zhao, X., Solano-Flores, G. and Qian, M. (2018) International test comparisons: Reviewing translation error in different source language-target language combinations. *International Multilingual Research Journal* 12 (1), 17–27. doi: 10.1080/19313152.2017.1349527

Zwick, R., Sklar, J.C., Wakefield, G., Hamilton, C., Norman, A. and Folsom, D. (2008) Instructional tools in educational measurement and statistics (ITEMS) for school personnel: Evaluation of three web-based training modules. *Educational Measurement: Issues and Practice* 27 (2), 14–27.

Index

accessibility, 25–26
accommodations, 52, 56–62
approach
   holistic, 2, 7–8, 10, 13–19, 21–22, 24, 26, 74, 100, 125–126, 131–132
   integrated, 2, 3, 7–10, 26–27, 42, 67, 75, 76, 99, 118–120, 125–127, 131, 132
   traditional, monolingual, 1, 10–13, 26, 100, 119, 132
assessment
   diagnostic, 6–7, 68
   formative, 6–7, 68, 96, 99, 103, 106, 119, 120, 123
   summative, 6–7, 68

Basic Interpersonal Communication Skills (BICS), 33, 46–47
bilingual bias, 20–21, 90
bilingual education
   strong, 8, 29–31
   weak, 8, 29–31
biliteracy, 30–31, 52

Chaos and Complexity Theory, 15, 17–18
classifying
   multilinguals, 8–9, 126–129
Cognitive Academic Language Proficiency (CALP), 33, 46–47
community languages, 62, 65, 82
construct
   monolingual, 12, 13, 17
   multilingual, 18–26
Content and Language Integrated Learning (CLIL), 8, 29, 31–34
Criterion-referenced test, 81

Developmental Interdependence Hypothesis, 18, 48
dialect
   German, South Tyrolean, 40
   German Walser, 39
   speakers, 22
diversity, 3, 14, 16
Dynamic model of multilingualism, 16, 18

eliciting narratives, 86–88
evaluation, 4, 5, 7, 9, 36, 37, 42, 43, 52, 77, 85, 88, 128

fallacy, black-and-white, 3, 20, 132
feedback, 6, 7, 52, 85, 99, 106, 119
Finland, 29, 36–37, 40, 42
functional
   bilingualism, 65, 128
   multilingualism, 29, 36– 37, 39, 41, 65, 81–82, 128–129

Heritage language programmes, 31

immersion, 30–32, 34, 37, 38
inclusivity, 25
individual multilingualism, 4, 5, 88
INVALSI, 40–41, 44, 63–64, 128

language background, 1, 20, 23, 27, 43, 48, 49, 53, 62, 64–67, 69, 70, 72, 79–82, 85, 88, 91, 108–109, 112, 114–115, 117, 121, 125, 127–128
language exposure, 62–63
Language mode hypothesis, 15–16, 19
living environment, 2, 42, 49, 64, 66–67, 118, 126, 128–129

macrostructure, 88–92, 94, 100, 106, 112–113, 115, 118–122
microstructure, 88, 91–92, 94, 100, 106
monolingual bias, 13, 20
monolingualism, 3, 30–31, 67, 131–132
multicompetence, 15–16, 18–19
Multilingual Assessment Instrument for Narratives (MAIN), 9, 85, 89, 92, 93–95, 106
multilingual-by-design test, 24, 25, 70–73, 75, 78, 81, 119, 120
multilingual-by-translation test, 24, 70, 72, 75–76
multilingual turn, 14

narrative abilities, 9, 84–85, 88–89, 95, 99–100, 109, 111, 118–120, 122–124
narratives
  bilingual, 85, 90, 95, 119, 122
  multilingual, 9, 83–95, 96–124
native speaker norm, 13
normed instruments, 85–86
normed test, 63

PISA, 13, 37, 40–41, 60–61, 70, 77, 105
programmes
  bilingual, 4, 28, 29–31
  multilingual, 8, 11, 28, 34–36, 38–39, 42–45

scoring, 2, 3, 51, 79–81
scoring rubrics, 8, 33, 51, 52–54, 74–76, 79–80, 89
societal multilingualism, 4
South Tyrol, 3, 9, 18, 23, 27, 35, 40, 101
speed of learning, 5, 20, 46, 48, 64, 102, 123, 126

test
  administration, 2, 8, 24, 56–57, 60, 67, 78–79, 126
  design, 13, 67, 69, 73, 76, 78, 118–119, 126
  interpretation, 2, 6, 8–9, 66–67, 75, 80–82, 120, 126
test accommodations, 52, 56–57
test instructions
  bilingual, 8, 52
The Basque Country, 29, 36, 38–42, 53, 61
Threshold hypothesis, 48
transfer, 11, 90–91, 100, 123–124
translanguaging, 3, 12, 15–16, 19, 55, 71, 73, 119
Trentino-Alto Adige/Südtirol, 39, 40–42, 96, 103
trilingual education, 2, 27, 35–36, 42, 53, 78, 80, 123

validity, 25, 56–57, 59, 68–70, 72
Valle d'Aosta/Vallée d'Aoste, 39, 78
viability, 24–26

For Product Safety Concerns and Information please contact our EU Authorised Representative:

Easy Access System Europe

Mustamäe tee 50

10621 Tallinn

Estonia

gpsr.requests@easproject.com

www.ingramcontent.com/pod-product-compliance
Ingram Content Group UK Ltd.
Pitfield, Milton Keynes, MK11 3LW, UK
UKHW022218250326
4937IPUK00005B/48